Change in View

Change in View

Principles of Reasoning

Gilbert Harman

A Bradford Book
The MIT Press
Cambridge, Massachusetts
London, England

This book was set in Palatino by The MIT Press Computergraphics Department and printed and bound by Halliday Lithograph in the United States of America.

Library of Congress Cataloging-in-Publication Data

Harman, Gilbert.
  Change in view.
  "A Bradford book."
  Bibliography: p.
  Includes indexes.
  1. Reasoning. 2. Logic. 3. Belief and doubt.
I. Title.
BC177.H37 1986   160   85-18766
ISBN 0-262-08155-5

For Olivia

Contents

Acknowledgments

Some material in chapter 4 appeared as part of "Positive versus Negative Undermining in Belief Revision," *Nous* 18 (1984), 39–49, and is reprinted by the permission of the editor. An earlier verson of chapter 9 appeared as "Rational Action and the Extent of Intention," *Social Theory and Practice* 9 (1983), 123–141, copyright *Social Theory and Practice*.

I am indebted to Stewart Cohen, Daniel Dennett, Jon Doyle, Robert Stalnaker, and Stephen Stich for comments on an earlier version of the manuscript.

The writing of this book was made possible in part by a fellowship form the National Endowment for the Humanities and a leave of absence from my teaching duties at Princeton University.

Change in View

Chapter 1

A Plea for the Study of Reasoning

Reasoning as Reasoned Change in View

Intending to have Cheerios for breakfast, Mary goes to the cupboard. But she can't find any Cheerios. She decides that Elizabeth must have finished off the Cheerios the day before. So, she settles for Rice Krispies. In the process, Mary has modified her original intentions and beliefs.

This is a very simple case of reasoned change in view, an elementary example of reasoning. It has the following two features. First, not only does Mary's reasoning lead her to add new beliefs to her view, so that she comes to believe that there are no more Cheerios and that Elizabeth ate the last Cheerios yesterday, it also leads her to give up things she had been believing, so that she stops believing that there are Cheerios in the cupboard and that she will have some Cheerios for breakfast. Second, Mary's reasoning changes not only her beliefs but also her plans and intentions. Her reasoning leads her to abandon her intention to have Cheerios and to adopt the new plan of having Rice Krispies. In other words, her reasoning is not only "theoretical," affecting her beliefs, but also "practical," affecting her intentions and plans.

In saying this, I assume that Mary's reasoning can be separated into distinct segments of practical and theoretical reasoning. I make this assumption even though any given segment of reasoning is likely to affect both her beliefs and her intentions, since changes in her beliefs can affect her plans, and changes in her plans can affect her beliefs. When Mary stops believing there are any Cheerios left, she also stops intending to have Cheerios for breakfast. When she forms her intention to have Rice Krispies instead, she also comes to believe that she will be having Rice Krispies for breakfast. But I assume there is a difference between immediate changes that are "part of" a given segment of her reasoning and less immediate changes that are merely further effects of that segment of reasoning.

True, it is not easy to say when a change is "part of" a given segment of reasoning and when it is merely the result of reasoning. For example, it is not immediately obvious whether changes in desires are *ever* part of reasoning. (I discuss this question briefly in chapter 8.) Nevertheless, in what follows I assume there is a definite difference between immediate changes that are part of a given segment of reasoning and other less immediate changes that are merely further effects of it. And I also assume there is a distinction between theoretical and practical reasoning.

These assumptions suggest a further distinction between two sorts of rules of reasoning, corresponding to two possible phases in reasoning. On the one hand there is often a process of reflection in which one thinks about one's beliefs, plans, desires, etc. and envisions various possibilities in more or less detail. On the other hand there is the actual revising of one's view, which may or may not follow such a reflection. *Maxims of reflection*, as we might call them, say what to consider before revising one's view, for example, that one should consider carefully all the alternatives, with vivid awareness of relevant evidence of possible consequences of contemplated courses of action. On the other hand what we might call *principles of revision* concern the actual changes to be made, the changes that are actually "part of" the reasoned revision, saying such things as that one should make minimal changes in one's view that increase its coherence as much as possible while promising suitable satisfaction of one's ends.

Not all principles of psychological change are principles of revision in this sense, since not all changes are instances of reasoning. For example, it may be that changes in desires are not instances of reasoning, although these changes can occur as a result of reasoning. Even so, there may be general principles governing changes in desires. These would be principles of change that were not principles of revision in the relevant sense.

I don't want to suggest that one ever makes *conscious* use of principles of revision in changing one's view. One can reason without knowing what the relevant principles of revision are and it may well be that reasoning is a relatively automatic process whose outcome is not under one's control.

In the rest of this book I explore the hypothesis that there is a difference between theoretical and practical reasoning and that principles of revision can be distinguished from principles of reflection and from other principles of change in view. For the time being I simply assume that there is something about some changes in view that makes it reasonable to call these changes "instances of reasoning" and to call the relevant principles "rules of revision," distinguishing these changes from others that are significantly different. This assumption seems initially plausible. I will try to show that it is also fruitful.

Reasoning Distinguished from Argument or Proof

Reasoned change in view like Mary's does not seem to have been studied much except for some recent research into planning and "belief revision" in the field of artificial intelligence (e.g., Doyle 1980). One possible cause of this otherwise general neglect is that reasoning in this sense may often be conflated with reasoning in another sense, namely argument for, or proof of, a conclusion from premises via a series of intermediate steps.

Old View $\xrightarrow{\text{Reasoning}}$ New View

```
         ————————
A        ————————       Premises
r        ————————
g
u        ——————
m        ————————
                        Intermediate Steps
e        ————————
n        ——————
t
         ————————       Final Conclusion
```

Clearly, argument or proof is not at all the same sort of thing as reasoning in the sense of reasoned change in view. There is a clear difference in category. Rules of argument are principles of implication, saying that propositions (or statements) of such and such a sort imply propositions (or statements) of such and such other sort. Consider the following principle:

Modus Ponens: P and *if P then Q* taken together imply *Q*.

Such a rule by itself says nothing at all in particular about belief revision. It may be that some principles of belief revisions *refer* to such principles of argument, that is, to principles of implication. It is an important issue in the theory of reasoning, conceived as change in view, just how implication or argument may be relevant to reasoning. I discuss this issue at some length in chapter 2. My present point is simply to note that rules of argument are not by themselves rules for revising one's view.

This difference in category between rules of implication and, as we might say, rules of inference (rules of revision) lies behind other differences between proof or argument and reasoning. For example, implication is *cumulative* in a way that inference may not be. In argument one accumulates conclusions; things are always added, never subtracted. Reasoned revision, however, can subtract from one's view as well as add to it. In order to express this point, the artificial intelligence work I have mentioned contrasts "monotonic reasoning," as in the usual sort of argument or proof, which is cumulative, with "nonmonotonic reasoning," as in ordinary reasoning or reasoned revision, which is not cumulative (Doyle 1980, 1982). But, although this terminology emphasizes the noncumulative character of reasoned revision, it is also potentially misleading in calling the ordinary sort of proof or argument "monotonic reasoning," because proof or argument is not of the same category as reasoned revision.

Induction and Deduction

Making a clear distinction between reasoning in the sense of reasoned change in view and reasoning in the sense of proof or argument can have a profound effect on how we view a variety of issues. For example, we might be led to question whether there are such things as "inductive arguments." These would be like "deductive arguments" except that the conclusion of an inductive argument would not have to follow logically from the premises, as in a deductive argument, but would only have to follow probabilistically (Black 1958).

Such inductive arguments would be "defeasible," that is, adding "premises" to an inductive argument might undercut the "validity" of the argument in a way that cannot happen with deductive arguments. For example, suppose that there is a valid or warranted inductive argument of the following form.

> Most F's are G's.
> Y is an F.
> So, Y is a G.

The "conclusion" here is not a deductive consequence of the premises; it can only be "made probable" by them. Adding premises in this case *can* undercut the argument. Suppose that we are given the following two additional premises:

> Most FH's are not G's.
> Y is an H.

Now the argument is the following:

> Most F's are G's.
> Y is an F.

Most *FH*'s are not *G*'s.
Y is an *H*.
So, *Y* is a *G*.

At this point, it may well be that the conclusion is no longer made probable by all the premises; so the argument from the extended set of premises would not be inductively valid (Hempel 1960).

Rules of inductive argument would be rules of "inductive logic" as opposed to deductive logic. It happens, however, that there is no well-developed enterprise of inductive logic in the way that there is for deductive logic.

Now, why should we think there are inductive arguments and an inductive logic? It is clear enough that there is something that might be called inductive reasoning, that is, inductively reasoned change in view. But if we clearly distinguish reasoned change in view from argument, we cannot suppose that the existence of inductive reasoning by itself shows there is such a thing as inductive argument, nor can we suppose that it shows there is an inductive logic.

Indeed, if we clearly distinguish reasoning from argument, we cannot suppose that the existence of deductive arguments shows there is such a thing as deductive reasoning, that is, deductively reasoned change in view. As I have already observed, rules of deduction are rules of deductive argument; they are not rules of inference or reasoning. They are not rules saying how to change one's view. Nor (to anticipate the discussion of this issue in chapter 2) are they easily matched to such rules. Consider again modus ponens. This principle does not say that, if one believes *P* and also believes *if P then Q*, then one can infer *Q*, because that is not always so. Sometimes one should give up *P* or *if P then Q* instead.

Even if some sort of principle of belief revision corresponded to this logical principle, the principle of belief revision would have to be a different principle. For one thing, the logical principle holds without exception, whereas there would be exceptions to the corresponding principle of belief revision. Mary believes that if she looks in the cupboard, she will see a box of Cheerios. She comes to believe that she is looking in the cupboard and that she does not see a box of Cheerios. At this point, Mary's beliefs are jointly inconsistent and therefore *imply* any proposition whatsoever. This does not authorize Mary to *infer* any proposition whatsoever. Nor does Mary infer whatever she might wish to infer. Instead she abandons her first belief, concluding that it is false after all.

Furthermore, even before Mary fails to find any Cheerios in the cupboard, it would be silly for her to clutter her mind with vast numbers of useless logical implications of her beliefs, such as *either she will have Cheerios for breakfast or the moon is made of green cheese.*

If there is a connection between standard principles of logic and principles of reasoning, it is not immediately obvious. There is a gap. We can't just state principles of logic and suppose that we have said something precise about reasoning. (I discuss the relation between logic and reasoning in chapter 2.)

Clearly, distinguishing between reasoning and argument can make one skeptical of the familiar idea that deduction and induction are different species of the same sort of thing. Obviously, there is deductive argument, but it is not similarly obvious that there is deductive reasoning. Again, it is not clear that there is such a thing as inductive argument, although we might say there is inductive reasoning. (It might be safer, however, to speak of theoretical reasoning instead of inductive reasoning, because theoretical reasoning contrasts with practical reasoning, which clearly exists, whereas to speak of inductive reasoning may suggest a contrast with deductive reasoning, which does not obviously exist.)

Analogous remarks also apply to the suggestion that there is such a thing as the practical syllogism (Anscombe 1957, p. 57). A syllogism is a form of argument, and although there is practical reasoning, there is not obviously any such thing as practical argument or logic and so not obviously any such thing as a practical syllogism.

Again, consider a defense of a "logic of entailment," which observes (1) in standard logic a contradiction logically implies any proposition at all, and (2) one is not justified in responding to the discovery that one's view is inconsistent by inferring anything whatsoever, concluding that (3) a new logic is needed (Meyer 1971). This line of thought loses plausibility if rules of inference or reasoning are distinguished from rules of implication or argument.

Finally, distinguishing reasoning from argument can make one worry that the work in artificial intelligence I have previously mentioned may be hampered by the so far unsuccessful search for principles of a non-monotonic logic, in contrast to the usual principles of monotonic logic (McCarthy 1980; McDermott and Doyle 1980; Reiter 1980). It may be a mistake to expect principles of reasoning to take the form of a logic.

In short, distinguishing reasoning from argument can make one suspicious of certain arguments for inductive logic, practical syllogisms, a logic of entailment, and so on. It is unclear how work on such "logics" might contribute to the study of reasoned revision.

Descriptive versus Normative Theories

My aim in this book is to contribute to the development of a theory of reasoned revision, but I find it hard to say whether the theory I want is a *normative* theory or a *descriptive* theory. A normative theory says how people *ought* to reason, whereas a descriptive theory says how they actually *do* reason. The theory I envision tries to say either or both of these things.

Actually, normative and descriptive theories of reasoning are intimately related. For one thing, as we will see, it is hard to come up with convincing normative principles except by considering how people actually do reason, which is the province of a descriptive theory. On the other hand it seems that any descriptive theory must involve a certain amount of idealization, and idealization is always normative to some extent.

The distinction between a normative and a descriptive theory seems as clear as the thought that one might sometimes reason in a way in which one ought not to have reasoned, in which case there is something wrong with one's reasoning. So let us consider ways in which one can make mistakes while reasoning. There are at least four such ways:

1. One might start with false beliefs and by reasoning be led into further errors.
2. One might reach a conclusion that is perfectly "reasonable," even though it happens to be mistaken.
3. One can be careless or inattentive; one can forget about a relevant consideration or fail to give it sufficient weight; one can make mistakes in long division; one can fail to see something, to remember something, to attend carefully; and so on.
4. One can revise one's view in accordance with an incorrect rule of revision, thereby violating the correct rules.

Mistakes of type 1 or 2 do not seem to be errors of reasoning at all. Only mistakes of type 3 and 4 seem to be errors of reasoning. Mistakes of type 3 seem to be mistakes of "reflection," involving the violation of a maxim of reflection. Mistakes of type 4 would be mistakes of revision, involving the violation of a principle of revision.

I envision a theory that says something about principles of revision. One way to try to discover the *right* principles of revision might be to consider actual cases in which people make mistakes of type 4 to see why they are mistakes. Through seeing when the wrong principles are followed, we might hope to discover what the right principles are. But it is not easy to find cases in which people clearly change their views in accordance with incorrect principles of revision. It is difficult to come up with an example that cannot be attributed instead to a mistaken belief, perhaps due to carelessness, so that the mistake is of type 1 and possibly type 3, rather than of type 4.

We cannot simply say one makes a mistake of type 4 whenever one reasons "fallaciously" in accordance with an "invalid" rule for changing one's view. If we distinguish clearly between argument and reasoning, we must agree that only arguments and proofs can be valid or invalid and that the notions of validity and invalidity have no clear application to changes in view, except in the sense that one can make a mistake about what validly implies what, a mistake that affects one's reasoning.

It is often said that there is a fallacy of "affirming the consequent," in which one reasons from the premises *if P then Q* and *Q* to the conclusion *P*. This would contrast with "affirming the antecedent," that is, modus ponens. But how are we to understand the contrast? Given a sharp distinction between reasoning and argument, we cannot suppose one's reasoning is valid if it proceeds in accordance with modus ponens and invalid if it proceeds in accordance with the principle of affirming the consequent. Modus ponens is a principle of argument or implication, not a principle of reasoned revision. If there is a "fallacy" here, it seems to involve making a type 1 mistake about what implies what.

Similar remarks apply to the so-called Gambler's Fallacy. This occurs, for example, in the game of roulette, in which one bets on where a spinning wheel with a pointer will stop. The pointer might end up on red or black (or very occasionally on green) and is equally likely to stop with the pointer on red as it is to stop with the pointer on black; that is, each time, the probability of red is the same as the probability of black. The Gambler's Fallacy consists in thinking that, under these conditions, red and black should each occur about half the time in any sufficiently long series of spins; so, if black has come up ten times in a row, red must be highly probable next time. This is a fallacy since it overlooks how the impact of an initial run of one color can become more and more insignificant as the sequence gets longer. If red and black occur each about half the time in a *long enough* sequence, they also occur about half the time in the somewhat longer sequence that includes ten extra occurrences of black at the beginning. For example, suppose red and black each occur 50% of the time in a sequence of 1000 spins of the wheel. Then in the longer sequence obtained by adding ten occurrences of black at the beginning, red and black each occur within half a percent of 50% of the time.

It may well turn out that all "fallacies" are best thought of either as mistakes of type 1, namely, reasoning from false beliefs in which the beliefs happen to be beliefs about what implies what or beliefs about probability, or as mistakes of type 3, involving carelessness or a failure to consider all the relevant possibilities. None of the fallacies clearly involves a distinctive mistake of type 4, in which a mistaken principle of change in view is followed. So, it seems that we cannot immediately use the existence of such fallacies to help us discover what the correct principles of revision are.

How then are we to begin to figure out what these principles of revision are? There seem to be two possible approaches. We can begin by considering how people actually *do* reason, by trying to figure out what principles they *actually follow*. Or we can begin with our "intuitions" as *critics* of reasoning. In either case we can then hope to find general principles. This will almost certainly involve some idealization. The suggested general principles will not coincide perfectly with our actual practice or with our intuitions about cases. This may lead us to modify the general principles, but it may also lead us to change our reasoning practice and/or our intuitions about what reasoning is correct. This can lead to a process of mutual adjustment of principles to practice and/or intuitions, a process of adjustment which can continue until we have reached what Rawls (1971) calls a reflective equilibrium. Furthermore, and this is important, we can also consider what rationale there might be for various principles we come up with and that can lead to further changes in principles, practices, and/or intuitions.

To repeat, even if we start by considering how people actually do reason, our account will probably have to involve a certain amount of idealization. Now, some kinds of idealization yield a normative theory, a notion of how one would reason if everything went right. So even this approach may yield a natural distinction between *is* and *ought*, between how things *do* happen and how they *ought* to happen. Indeed, it may do so in more than one way.

In what follows I consider matters from both the viewpoint of our intuitions as critics and the viewpoint of our actual practice. These two approaches yield somewhat different results. As we will see, the appeal to intuition tends toward a greater degree of idealization. In particular, it tends to overlook or minimize practical limitations, such as limitations on memory or on calculative capacity. What seems wrong when these limitations are not taken into account may be quite reasonable when they are taken into account. So the two approaches can seem at least initially to yield different results.

Human versus Artificial Reasoning

I am concerned with human reasoning, given the constraints of human psychology. Although occasionally I allude to work in artificial intelligence, I am here concerned with this work not for its own sake but only for the light it may shed on human reasoning.

My conclusions about human reasoning may sometimes be relevant to work in artificial intelligence. For example, I argue in chapter 3 that people cannot do much probabilistic reasoning because of a combinatorial explosion such reasoning involves. If this is correct, the same limitation will apply to the "reasoning" of artificial intelligence systems. But human reasoning is affected by other limits to which artificial intelligence may not be subject, for example, limits on short-term memory. Seeing how humans reason in consquence of *these* limits may or may not be of much interest for artificial intelligence.

Summary

I am concerned with reasoned change in view. Such reasoning may involve giving up things previously accepted as well as coming to accept new things. I assume there is a difference between theoretical reasoning, which immediately modifies beliefs, and practical reasoning, which immediately modifies plans and intentions. I also assume we can distinguish maxims of reflection, saying what to think about before revising one's view, from principles of revision, the rules concerning the actual revision to be made.

Reasoning in the sense of reasoned change in view should never be identified with proof or argument; inference is not implication. Logic is the theory of implication, not directly the theory of reasoning. Although we can say there is inductive reasoning, it is by no means obvious that there is any such thing as inductive argument or inductive logic. Nor does the existence of practical reasoning show there is such a thing as a practical syllogism or a practical logic.

Finally, it is not at this point easy to distinguish a descriptive theory of reasoned revision from a normative theory. Any normative investigation must begin by considering how people actually do reason and how people criticize reasoning. Any descriptive theory has to make use of idealization.

Chapter 2

Logic and Reasoning

Even if they agree that logic is not by itself a theory of reasoning, many people will be inclined to suppose that logic has some sort of special relevance to the theory of reasoning. In this chapter I argue that this inclination should be resisted. It turns out that logic is not of any special relevance.

Implications, Inconsistency, and Practical Limits

If logic does have special relevance to reasoning, it would seem that its relevance must be captured at least roughly by the following two principles.

> *Logical Implication Principle* The fact that one's view logically implies *P* can be a reason to accept *P*.

> *Logical Inconsistency Principle* Logical inconsistency is to be avoided.

These are distinct principles. Suppose one believes both *P* and also *if P then Q*. Since these beliefs imply *Q*, the Logical Implication Principle says this may give one a reason to believe *Q*. It does not say one should also refrain from believing *Q*'s denial, *not Q*. Believing *not Q* when one also believes *P* and *if P then Q* is contrary to the Logical Inconsistency Principle, not to the Logical Implication Principle. On the other hand the Logical Inconsistency Principle does not say one has a reason to believe *Q* given that one believes *P* and *if P then Q*.

Neither principle is exceptionless as it stands. Each holds, as it were, other things being equal. Each is defeasible. For example, the Logical Implication Principle entails that, if one believes both *P* and *if P then Q*, that can be a reason to believe *Q*. But, clearly, that is not *always* a reason to believe *Q*, since sometimes when one believes *P* and also believes *if P then Q*, one should *not* come to believe *Q*. Remember Mary who came to believe three inconsistent things: If she looks in the closet she will see a box of Cheerios, she is looking in the closet, but she does not see a box of Cheerios. Mary should not at this point infer that she does see a box of Cheerios from her first two beliefs.

This suggests modifying the Logical Implication Principle:

> *Logical Closure Principle*   One's beliefs should be "closed under logical implication." In other words there is something wrong with one's beliefs if there is a proposition logically implied by them which one does not already believe. In that case one should either add the implied proposition to one's beliefs or give up one of the implying beliefs.

But the Logical Closure Principle is not right either. Many trivial things are implied by one's view which it would be worse than pointless to add to what one believes. For example, if one believes P, one's view trivially implies "either P or Q," "either P or P," "P and either P or R," and so on. There is no point in cluttering one's mind with all these propositions. And, of course, there are many other similar examples.

Here I am assuming the following principle:

> *Clutter Avoidance*   One should not clutter one's mind with trivialities.

This raises an interesting issue. To suppose one's mind could become cluttered with beliefs is to suppose such things as (1) that it takes time to add to one's beliefs further propositions that are trivially implied by them, time that might be better spent on other things, and/or (2) that one has "limited storage capacity" for beliefs, so there is a limit on the number of things one can believe, and/or (3) that there are limits on "information retrieval," so the more one believes the more difficult it is to recall relevant beliefs when one needs them.

Such suppositions presuppose that beliefs are explicitly "represented" in the mind in the sense that these representations play the important role in perception, thought, and reasoning that we think beliefs play.

But we must be careful in stating this presupposition. Not all one's beliefs can be explicitly represented in this way, since then one could believe only finitely many things. But one can and does believe infinitely many things. For example, one believes the earth does not have two suns, the earth does not have three suns, the earth does not have four suns, and so on.

In order to accommodate this point, I assume that we can distinguish what one believes *explicitly* from what one believes only *implicitly*. Then we can take the principle of clutter avoidance to apply to what one believes explicitly.

Explicit and Implicit Belief

I assume one believes something explicitly if one's belief in that thing involves an explicit mental representation whose content is the content of that belief. On the other hand something is believed only implicitly if it is not explicitly believed but, for example, is easily inferable from one's explicit beliefs. Given that one explicitly believes the earth has exactly one sun, one can easily infer that the earth does not have two suns, that the earth does not have three suns, and so on. So all these propositions are things one believes implicitly.

That is an example in which implicit beliefs are implied by explicit beliefs. There are also cases in which one implicitly believes something that is easily inferable from one's beliefs without being strictly implied by them. An example might be one's implicit belief that elephants don't wear pajamas in the wild (Dennett 1978).

There is also another way in which something can be implicitly believed—it may be implicit in one's believing something else. For example, in explicitly believing P, it may be that one implicitly believes one is justified in believing P. The proposition that one is justified in believing P is not ordinarily implied by the proposition P and may not be inferable from one's explicit beliefs, but it may be that in believing P one is committed to and so implicitly believes the proposition that one is justified by believing P. (I discuss this and related possibilities in chapter 5.)

It is a possible view that *none* of one's beliefs are explicit, that is, that none are explicitly represented and all are only implicit in one's mental makeup. This is a form of behaviorism about belief. There is surprisingly much that can be said in favor of such behaviorism (Dennett 1978; Stalnaker 1984), but I suppose that whatever is ultimately the right view of belief must allow that unbridled inference can lead to too much clutter either in what one explicitly *believes* or in whatever explicit thing underlies belief. Therefore I ignore the possibility of such behaviorism and continue to assume that one's implicit beliefs are implicit in one's believing certain things explicitly. If this is wrong, I doubt that it is so wrong as to affect the conclusions I draw from this assumption.

In this connection it might be useful for me to digress briefly to observe that the distinction between explicit and implicit belief is not the same as either the distinction between belief that is available to consciousness and unconscious belief or that between "occurrent" and "dispositional" beliefs.

We normally consider a belief "unconscious" if one is not aware one has it and one cannot easily become aware of it simply by considering whether one has it. Otherwise the belief is available to consciousness. Now, clearly, implicit beliefs can be available to consciousness. The belief that the earth does not have two suns is normally only implicit in one's explicit beliefs and is not itself explicitly represented, even though it is immediately available to consciousness in the sense that, if one considers whether one believes it, one can immediately tell one does.

On the other hand a belief can be explicitly represented in one's mind, written down in Mentalese as it were, without necessarily being available to consciousness. For example, one might explicitly believe that one's mother does not love one, even though this belief may not be consciously retrievable without extensive psychoanalysis. So the distinction between implicit and explicit beliefs is not the same as that between unconscious beliefs and those available to consciousness.

Turning now to the distinction between occurrent and dispositional beliefs, we can say a belief is occurrent if it is either currently before one's consciousness or in some other way currently operative in guiding what one is thinking or doing. A belief is merely dispositional if it is only potentially occurrent in this sense. Any merely implicit belief is merely dispositional, but explicit beliefs are not always occurrent, since only some explicit beliefs are currently operative at any given time. So the distinction between implicit and explicit beliefs is not the same as that between occurrent and dispositional beliefs.

So much for this digression comparing these various distinctions in kinds of beliefs.

Let me return to the discussion of the Logical Closure Principle, which says one's beliefs should be closed under logical implication. Clearly this principle does not apply to explicit beliefs, since one has only a finite number of explicit beliefs and they have infinitely many logical consequences. Nor can the Logical Closure Principle be satisfied even by one's implicit beliefs. One cannot be expected even implicitly to believe a logical consequence of one's beliefs if a complex proof would be needed to see the implication.

It won't help to change the Logical Closure Principle to say one's beliefs should be closed under *obvious* logical implication. That would come to the same thing, since any logical implication can eventually be demonstrated by a proof consisting entirely of a series of obvious steps. This means that, if beliefs are required to be closed under obvious logical implication, they are required to be closed under any logical implication, obvious or not. So, since beliefs cannot be required to be closed under logical implication, they cannot be required to be closed under obvious logical implication either.

Clutter Avoidance

How is the principle of clutter avoidance to be used? It seems absurd for it to figure explicitly in one's reasoning, so that one refrains from drawing an otherwise acceptable conclusion on the grounds of clutter avoidance. Once one is explicitly considering whether or not to accept a conclusion, one cannot decide not to on such grounds. One might rationally decide not to try to remember it, perhaps, but one cannot decide not to believe it at least for the moment.

Suppose George is trying to convince Bob that *P*. George shows how *P* is a deductive consequence of things Bob believes. Bob accepts the validity of George's argument and refuses to change his belief in any of the premises, but he also refuses to accept the conclusion *P*, citing clutter avoidance as his reason for refusing. That is absurd. (I am indebted to Robert Stalnaker for this example.)

But the Principle of Clutter Avoidance is not just a principle about what one should try to remember. It would be a violation of clutter avoidance if one spent all one's time thinking up trivial consequences of one's beliefs even if one refrained from committing these consequences to memory. In that case one would be cluttering up one's short-term processing capacities with trivialities.

The Principle of Clutter Avoidance is a metaprinciple that constrains the actual principles of revision. The principles of revision must be such that they discourage a person from cluttering up either long-term memory or short-term processing capacities with trivialities. One way to do this would be to allow one to accept a new belief *P* only if one has (or ought to have) an interest in whether *P* is true. (This is discussed in chapter 6.)

Unavoidable Inconsistency and the Liar Paradox

I was saying that neither the Logical Implication Principle nor the Inconsistency Principle is without exception. I have indicated why this is so for the Logical Implication Principle, which says one has a reason to believe the logical implications of one's beliefs. Similar remarks hold for the Logical Inconsistency Principle, which says one should avoid inconsistency.

To see that the Logical Inconsistency Principle has its exceptions, observe that sometimes one discovers one's views are inconsistent and does not know how to revise them in order to avoid inconsistency without great cost. In that case the best response may be to keep the inconsistency and try to avoid inferences that exploit it. This happens in everyday life whenever one simply does not have time to figure out what to do about a discovered inconsistency. It can also happen on more reflective occasions. For example, there is the sort of inconsistency that arises when one believes that not all one's beliefs could be true. One might well be justified in continuing to believe that and each of one's other beliefs as well.

There are also famous logical paradoxes. For example, the liar paradox involves reflection on the following remark, which I call (L):

(L) is not true.

Thinking about (L) leads one into contradiction. If (L) is not true, things are as (L) says, so (L) must be true. But if (L) is true, then it is true that (L) is not true, so (L) must not be true. It seems (L) is true if and only if (L) is not true. But that is a contradiction.

The paradox arises from our uncritical acceptance of the following:

Biconditional Truth Schema   "P" is true if and only if P.

To see that this schema is indeed the culprit, notice that one instance of it is

"(L) is not true" is true if and only if (L) is not true.

Since (L) = "(L) is not true," this instance is equivalent to the self-contradictory

(L) is true if and only if (L) is not true

Various restrictions on the Biconditional Truth Schema have been suggested in order to avoid the liar paradox, but none is completely satisfactory (Kripke 1975, Herzberger 1982). So, the rational response for most of us may simply be to recognize our beliefs about truth are logically inconsistent, agree this is undesirable, and try not to exploit this inconsistency in our inferences. (The danger is that, since inconsistent beliefs logically imply anything, if one is not careful, one will be able to use this fact to infer anything whatsoever.)

In practice the best solution may be to retain the Biconditional Truth Schema and yet avoid contradiction by interpreting the Schema not as something that holds without exception but rather as something that holds "normally" or "other things being equal." It is then a "default assumption." One accepts any given instance of the Biconditional Truth Schema in the absence of a sufficiently strong reason not to accept it. One does not apply the Schema to (L) because doing so leads to contradiction.

This does not seem to be a satisfactory solution from the point of view of logic, since we take logic to require precise principles with precise boundaries, not principles that hold merely "normally" or "other things being equal." But in ordinary life we accept many principles of this vaguer sort.

My point about the Logical Inconsistency Principle remains. One may find oneself with inconsistent beliefs and not have the time or ability to trace the sources of the inconsistency (e.g., the Biconditional Truth Schema). In that event, it is rational simply to retain the contradictory beliefs, trying not to exploit the inconsistency.

Immediate Implication and Immediate Inconsistency

I turn now to an issue about the Logical Implication and Inconsistency Principles I have so far mentioned only in passing. One might have *no* reason to accept something that is logically implied by one's beliefs if there is no short and simple argument showing this. To take an extreme example, one accepts basic principles of arithmetic that logically imply some unknown proposition P which is the answer to an unsolved mathematical problem: but one has no reason to believe P if one is not aware that P is implied by these basic principles. This suggests revising the Logical Implication Principle:

> *Recognized Logical Implication Principle*   One has a reason to believe P if one *recognizes* that P is logically implied by one's view.

Similarly, we might revise the Logical Inconsistency Principle:

> *Recognized Logical Inconsistency Principle*   One has a reason to avoid believing things one recognizes to be logically inconsistent.

However, there is a problem with this. It would seem one can *recognize* a logical implication or logical inconsistency only if one has the relevant concept of logical implication or logical inconsistency. But it would seem that few people have such concepts, at least if this involves distinguishing logical implication and inconsistency from other sorts of implication and inconsistency. Consider the following examples:

> *P* or *Q* and *not P* taken together imply *Q*.
> $A = B$ and $B = C$ taken together imply $A = C$.
> $A < B$ and $B < C$ taken together imply $A < C$.
> *A is part of B* and *B is part of C* taken together imply *A is part of C*.
> *X is Y's brother* implies *X is male*.
> *Today is Thursday* implies *Tomorrow is Friday*.
> *X plays defensive tackle for the Philadelphia Eagles* implies *X weighs more than 150 pounds*.

People who recognize these and related implications do not in any consistent way distinguish them into purely logical implications and others that are not purely logical. (Only the first counts as purely logical in "classical" first-order predicate logic without identity. Sometimes principles for identity are included as part of logic, in which the second also counts as a logical implication.) So the Recognized Logical Implication and Inconsistency Principles would seem to have only a limited application.

To some extent this objection can be met by generalizing the principles, dropping specific mention of logical implication and inconsistency. Then the principles would be stated as follows:

Recognized Implication Principle   One has a reason to believe *P* if one recognizes that *P* is implied by one's view.

Recognized Inconsistency Principle   One has a reason to avoid believing things one recognizes to be inconsistent.

These principles still apply only to people who have concepts of implication and inconsistency. But this is not so clearly problematical, if only because it is not clear what it takes to have these concepts.

I suggest it is enough to be able to make reasoned changes in one's view in a way that is sensitive to implication and inconsistency. Someone who is disposed to treat beliefs in *P* and *if P then Q* as reasons to believe *Q* has, by virtue of that very disposition, an appropriate ability to recognize this sort of implication, at least if this disposition is also accompanied by the disposition not to believe *P*, *if P then Q*, and *not Q*. And the latter sort of disposition might reflect an appropriate ability to recognize that sort of inconsistency.

I am inclined to take as fundamental certain dispositions to treat propositions in certain ways, in particular, dispositions to treat some propositions as *immediately implying* others and some as *immediately inconsistent* with each other. That is, I am inclined to suppose that the basic notions are

$P, Q, \ldots, R$ immediately imply S for A

and

$P, Q, \ldots, R$ are immediately inconsistent for A.

It is unclear to me whether these notions can be reduced to others in any interesting way. (I am indebted to Scott Soames for raising this issue.) If *A* is disposed to treat some beliefs as implying others, then *A* is disposed to treat beliefs that immediately imply something as giving him or her a reason to believe that thing; but we cannot *identify*

$P, Q, \ldots, R$ immediately imply S for A

with

A is disposed to treat $P, Q, \ldots, R$ as a reason to believe S.

For one thing, A's general disposition may be overridden by other considerations in a particular case, for example, if S is absurd. In that case, some of A's beliefs will immediately imply a particular proposition for A, although A is not disposed to treat those beliefs as reasons for believing that proposition. Furthermore, beliefs can be treated by A as *reasons* for believing a conclusion even though A does not take those beliefs to *imply* that conclusion.

Similarly, we can say A is disposed to avoid believing things that are immediately inconsistent for A but we cannot identify a set of beliefs' being inconsistent for A with A's having a disposition to avoid believing all the members of that set. On the one hand the general disposition may be overridden in a particular case, as when A is disposed to believe the premises of the liar paradox. On the other hand (as Soames observes) there is Moore's paradox: One is strongly disposed not to believe both P and that one does not believe P while realizing that these propositions are perfectly consistent with each other.

So, I am inclined simply to assume one has certain basic dispositions to take some propositions immediately to imply other propositions and to take some propositions as immediately inconsistent with each other. More generally, I assume one can have general dispositions with respect to certain patterns of immediate implication and inconsistency even if some instances of the patterns are so long or complex or otherwise distracting that one has no particular disposition to take those particular instances to be immediate implications or inconsistencies.

Summary and Conclusion

I began by suggesting logic might be specially relevant to reasoning in two ways, via implication and inconsistency. It seemed the relevant principles would be defeasible, holding only other things being equal. Furthermore, they would apply only to someone who recognized the implication or inconsistency. Since this recognition might be manifested simply in the way a person reacts to these implications and inconsistencies, I suggested that certain implications and inconsistencies are "immediate" for a given person. (In appendix A, I discuss whether basic logical notions can be defined in terms of such immediate implications and inconsistencies. I also discuss the hypothesis that only logical implications and inconsistencies are immediate and that others are mediated by the acceptance of certain nonlogical principles, concluding that this hypothesis may be impossible to refute.)

My conclusion is that there is no clearly significant way in which *logic* is specially relevant to reasoning. On the other hand immediate *implication* and immediate *inconsistency* do seem important for reasoning, and so do implication and inconsistency. Sometimes, reasoning culminates in the conclusion that a certain argument is a good one or that certain propositions are inconsistent. But that is not to say that logical implication or logical inconsistency has any special status in human reasoning.

Chapter 3
Belief and Degree of Belief

Probabilistic Implication

We have a rule connecting implication and reasoning:

> *Principle of Immediate Implication*   That *P* is immediately implied by things one believes can be a reason to believe *P*.

Is there also a weaker probabilistic version of this rule?

> *Hypothetical Principle of Immediate Probabilistic Implication*   That *P* is obviously highly probable, given one's beliefs, can be a reason to believe *P*.

Suppose Mary purchases a ticket in the state lottery. Given her beliefs, it is obviously highly probable that her ticket will not be one of the winning tickets. Can she infer that her ticket will not win? Is she justified in believing her ticket is not one of the winning tickets?

Intuitions waver here. On the one hand, if Mary is justified in believing her ticket is not one of the winning tickets, how can she be justified in buying the ticket in the first place? Furthermore, it certainly seems wrong to say she can *know* that her ticket is not one of the winning tickets if it is really a fair lottery. On the other hand the probability that the ticket is not one of the winning tickets seems higher than the probability of other things we might easily say Mary knows. We ordinarily allow that Mary can come to know various things by reading about them in the newspaper, even though we are aware that newspapers sometimes get even important stories wrong.

This issue is one that I will return to several times, but I want to begin by considering a suggestion which I think is mistaken, namely, that the trouble here comes from not seeing that belief is a matter of degree.

All-or-Nothing Belief

I have been supposing that, for the theory of reasoning, explicit belief is an all-or-nothing matter. I have assumed that, as far as principles of reasoning are concerned, one either believes something explicitly or one does not; in other words an appropriate "representation" is either in one's "memory" or not. The principles of reasoning are principles for modifying such all-or-nothing representations.

This is not to deny that in some ways belief is a matter of degree. For one thing implicit belief is certainly a matter of degree, since it is a matter of how easily and automatically one can infer something from what one believes explicitly. Furthermore, explicit belief is a matter of degree in the sense that one believes some things more strongly than others. Sometimes one is only somewhat inclined to believe something, sometimes one is not sure what to believe, sometimes one is inclined to disbelieve something, sometimes one is quite confident something is not so, and so forth.

How should we account for the varying strengths of explicit beliefs? I am inclined to suppose that these varying strengths are implicit in a system of beliefs one accepts in a yes/no fashion. My guess is that they are to be explained as a kind of epiphenomenon resulting from the operation of rules of revision. For example, it may be that P is believed more strongly than Q if it would be harder to stop believing P than to stop believing Q, perhaps because it would require more of a revision of one's view to stop believing P than to stop believing Q.

In contrast to this, it might be suggested that principles of reasoning *should* be rules for modifying explicit *degrees of belief*. In this view, an account of reasoning should be embedded in a theory of subjective probability, for example, as developed by Jeffrey (1983), not that Jeffrey himself accepts this particular suggestion. In fact, this suggestion cannot really be carried out. People do not normally associate with their beliefs degrees of confidence of a sort they can use in reasoning. It is too complicated for them to do so. Degrees of belief are and have to be implicit rather than explicit, except for a few special cases of beliefs that are explicitly beliefs about probabilities.

Let me say why this is so. To begin with, Kyburg (1961) observes that the Immediate Implication and Inconsistency Principles would not be right even as approximations if belief were a matter of degree.

> *Immediate Implication Principle*   The fact that one's view immediately implies P can be a reason to accept P.

> *Immediate Inconsistency Principle*   Immediate logical inconsistency in one's view can be a reason to modify one's view.

Propositions that are individually highly probable can have an immediate implication that is not. The fact that one assigns a high probability to P and also to *if P then Q* is not a sufficient reason to assign a high probability to Q. Each premise of a valid argument might be probable even though the conclusion is improbable. Since one might assign a high degree of belief to various propositions without being committed to assigning a high degree of belief to a logical consequence of these propositions, Kyburg argues that the Logical Implication Principle is mistaken.

Similarly, each of an inconsistent set of beliefs might be highly probable. To take Kyburg's lottery example, it might be that the proposition, "one of the N tickets in this lottery is the winning ticket" is highly probable, and so is each proposition of the form, "ticket i is not the winning ticket," for each i between 1 and N. So one might believe each of these propositions to a high degree while recognizing that they are jointly inconsistent. Kyburg argues there is nothing wrong with this, so the Logical Inconsistency Principle is mistaken.

It is not just that these principles have exceptions. We have seen that they are defeasible and hold only other things being equal. But if belief were always a matter of degree the principles would not even hold in this way as defeasible principles. They would not hold at all.

It would be odd for someone to take this seriously in a routine matter. It is contrary to the way we normally think. Imagine arguing with such a person. You get him to believe certain premises and to appreciate that they imply your conclusion, but he is not persuaded to believe this conclusion, saying that, although you have persuaded him to assign a high probability to each of your premises, that is not enough to show he should assign a high probability to the conclusion! This is not the way people usually respond to arguments.

Or consider the following attitude toward contradiction. As Jack asserts several things, you observe that he has contradicted himself. His response is that he sees nothing wrong, since all the things he has asserted are highly probable. This is comprehensible, but it is again different from the normal way of doing things.

A normal reaction to someone's refusal to accept the conclusion of a clearly valid argument after he says he has been persuaded to accept the premises, if he gives Kyburg's reason, is to suppose that he does not really accept the premises after all, but only believes of each that it is probable. Similarly, we suppose that a person who says at least one ticket will win and also says of each ticket that it will not win does not really believe of each ticket that it will not win but merely believes of each ticket that it is unlikely that that ticket will win. We do not ordinarily think of this as like the case in which an author believes each of the things he or she says in a book he or she has written and also believes that, given human fallibility, at least one of the things he or she has said in the book must be false. Such a person is justified in having inconsistent beliefs, but that does not show that the Recognized Inconsistency Principle is incorrect. It only shows that the principle is defeasible.

Of course, to say one normally thinks of belief in an all-or-nothing way is not to deny one sometimes has beliefs about probabilities. More important, one often manifests a varying degree of confidence in this or that proposition as revealed in one's willingness to *act*, for example, to bet. But this does not show one normally or usually assigns *explicit* levels of confidence or probability to one's beliefs. The degree of confidence one has might be merely implicit in one's system of beliefs. Subjective probability theory can give an account of one's dispositions without being an account of the psychological reality underlying those dispositions.

It might be said one *ought* to operate using explicit degrees of belief. This would imply one should make much more use of probability theory than one does.

Similarly, it might be said that one's goals should be treated as matters of degree. Since different prospects are more or less desirable, one ought to assign them different degrees of "subjective utility." In acting, one should act so as to maximize expected utility.

In chapter 9 I argue that this is not right. But even if it were right, such an appeal to probability theory would not eliminate the need for reasoning in the sense of change in view. One's subjective probability assignments would never be complete. They would often have to be extended. To some extent they could be extended by means of the Principle of Immediate Implication by considering the immediate implications of one's current probability assignments and by allowing for clutter avoidance and other relevant considerations. Furthermore, there would also often be cases in which current subjective probability assignments would have to be changed, for example because they were not consistent with each other. The Principle of Immediate Inconsistency then has a role to play. And there are other cases in which one will want to modify such assignments, for example, when one discovers that a current theory would explain old evidence one had not realized it would explain (Glymour 1980, chap. 3). And whatever principles are developed for changing all-or-nothing belief will apply to changing degrees of belief, treating these as all-or-nothing beliefs about probabilities.

Conditionalization

Some probability theorists appear to deny these obvious points. They seem to suppose that reasoned revision is or ought always to be in accordance with a special principle of "conditionalization" that applies when one comes to treat evidence *E* as certain. The claim is that in such a case one is to modify one's other degrees of belief so that the new probability one assigns to any given proposition *P* is given by the following formula:

$$\text{new prob } (P) = \frac{\text{old prob } (P \ \& \ E)}{\text{old prob } (E)}$$

The quotient on the right-hand side is sometimes called the conditional probability of *P* given E, which is why the principle is called conditionalization.

R. C. Jeffrey (1983, chap. 11) shows how this formula can be generalized to allow for the case in which evidence propositions change in probability without becoming certain. Suppose that there are *n* relevant atomic evidence propositions $E_1, \ldots, E_n$, so that there are 2^n strongest conjunctions C_i each containing E_i or its denial. Then the new probability one assigns to any given proposition *P* is the sum of all the quantities of the following form:

$$\text{new prob } (C_i) \times \frac{\text{old prob } (P \ \& \ C_i)}{\text{old prob } (C_i)}$$

So, let us consider the following hypothesis, which is widely accepted by subjective probability theorists:

Reasoning is conditionalization   The updating of probabilities via conditionalization or generalized conditionalization is (or ought to be) the only principle of reasoned revision.

One way to argue for this is to try to show that various intuitively acceptable principles of reasoning from evidence can be accounted for if this hypothesis is accepted (e.g., Dorling 1972; Horwich 1982).

However, there is a problem with making extensive use of this method of updating. One can use conditionalization to get a new probability for *P* only if one has already assigned a prior probability not only to *E* but to *P* & *E*. If one is to be prepared for various possible conditionalizations, then for every proposition *P* one wants to update, one must already have assigned probabilities to various conjunctions of *P* together with one or more of the possible evidence propositions and/ or their denials. Unhappily, this leads to a combinatorial explosion, since the number of such conjunctions is an exponential function of the number of possibly relevant evidence propositions. In other words, to be prepared for coming to accept or reject any of ten evidence propositions, one would have to record probabilities of over a thousand such conjunctions for each proposition one is interested in updating. To be prepared for twenty evidence propositions, one must record a million probabilities. For thirty evidence propositions, a billion probabilities are needed, and so forth.

Clearly, one could not represent all the needed conjunctions explicitly. One would have to represent them implicitly using some sort of general principle. Given such a general principle, one's total probability distribution would then be determined, by either (1) the total evidence one accepts as certain (using conditionalization) or (2) the various new probabilities assigned to the C_i (using Jeffrey's generalization of conditionalization). But neither (1) nor (2) is feasible. Consider what is involved in each case.

The idea behind (1) is to represent the degrees of belief to which one is presently committed by means of some general principle, specifying an initial probability distribution, together with a list of all the evidence one has come to treat as certain. Such evidence will include all immediate perceptual evidence—how things look, sound, smell, etc., to one at this or that moment. One will have to remember all such evidence that has influenced one's present degrees of belief. But in fact one rarely remembers such evidence beyond the moment in which one possesses it (a point I return to in chapter 4). So (1) is not a usable approach.

On the other hand, (2) requires that one keep track of one's current degree of belief in each of the relevant conjunctions C_i of evidence propositions and/or their denials. These are things one does not have to be certain about, so the relevant propositions need not be for the most part about immediate perceptual experience, as in (1). So the objection that one hardly ever remembers such propositions does not apply to (2). But (2) is also unworkable, since the number of relevant conjunctions C_i is an exponential function of the number of atomic evidence propositions.

These objections assume one sticks with one's original general principle describing one's initial degrees of belief and records one's present degrees of belief by representing the new evidence accepted as certain or the new probabilities of the various conjunctions C_i.

Alternatively, one might try each time to find a new principle describing one's updated degrees of belief in a single general statement. But the problem of finding such a general principle is intractable, and anyway (b) there will normally be no simpler way to describe one's new probability distribution than the description envisioned in (1) or (2), so this will not normally be feasible either.

Doing extensive updating by conditionalization or generalized conditionalization would be too complicated in practice. Therefore one must follow other principles in revising one's views. It is *conceivable* that all or some of these principles might refer to strength or degree of belief and not just to whether one believes something in a yes/no fashion. But the actual principles we follow do not seem to be of that sort, and it is unclear how these principles might be modified to be sensitive to degree or strength of belief. In the rest of this book I assume that, as far as the principles of revision we follow are concerned, belief is an all-or-nothing matter. I assume that this is so because it is too complicated for mere finite beings to make extensive use of probabilities.

Chapter 4
Positive versus Negative Undermining

I now want to compare two competing theories of reasoned belief revision, which I will call the foundations theory and the coherence theory since they are similar to certain philosophical theories of justification sometimes called foundations and coherence theories (Sosa 1980; Pollock 1979). But the theories I am concerned with are not precisely the same as the corresponding philosophical theories of justification, which are not normally presented as theories of belief revision. Actually, I am not sure what these philosophical theories of "justification" are supposed to be concerned with. So, although I will be using the *term* "justification" in what follows, as well as the terms "coherence" and "foundations," I do not claim that my use of any of these terms is the same as its use in these theories of justification. I mean to be raising a new issue, not discussing an old one.

The key issue is whether one needs to keep track of one's original justifications for beliefs. What I am calling the *foundations* theory says yes; what I am calling the *coherence* theory says no.

The foundations theory holds that some of one's beliefs "depend on" others for their current justification; these other beliefs may depend on still others, until one gets to foundational beliefs that do not depend on any further beliefs for their justification. In this view reasoning or belief revision should consist, first, in subtracting any of one's beliefs that do not now have a satisfactory justification and, second, in adding new beliefs that either need no justification or are justified on the basis of other justified beliefs one has.

On the other hand, according to the coherence theory, it is not true that one's ongoing beliefs have or ought to have the sort of justificational structure required by the foundations theory. In this view ongoing beliefs do not usually require any justification. Justification is taken to be required only if one has a special reason to doubt a particular belief. Such a reason might consist in a conflicting belief or in the observation that one's beliefs could be made more "coherent," that is, more organized or simpler or less ad hoc, if the given belief were abandoned (and perhaps if certain other changes were made). According to the coherence theory, belief revision should involve minimal changes in one's beliefs in a way that sufficiently increases overall coherence.

In this chapter I elaborate these two theories in order to compare them with actual reasoning and intuitive judgments about such reasoning. It turns out that the theories are most easily distinguished by the conflicting advice they occasionally give concerning whether one should *give up* a belief P from which many other of one's beliefs have been inferred, when P's original justification has to be abandoned. Here a surprising contrast seems to emerge—"is" and "ought" seem to come apart. The foundations theory seems, at least at first, to be more in line with our intuitions about how people *ought* to revise their beliefs; the coherence theory is more in line with what people *actually do* in such situations. Intuition seems strongly to support the foundations theory over the coherence theory as an account of what one is *justified* in doing in such cases; but *in fact* one will tend to act as the coherence theory advises.

After I explain this I consider how this apparent discrepancy can be resolved. I conclude that the coherence theory is normatively correct after all, despite initial appearances.

The Foundations Theory of Belief Revision

The basic principle of the foundations theory, as I will interpret it, is that one must keep track of one's original reasons for one's beliefs, so that one's ongoing beliefs have a justificational structure, some beliefs serving as reasons or justifications for others. These justifying beliefs are more basic or fundamental for justification than the beliefs they justify.

The foundations theory rejects any principle of *conservatism*. In this view a proposition cannot acquire justification simply by being believed. The justification of a given belief cannot be, either in whole or in part, that one has that belief. For example, one's justification for believing something cannot be that one already believes it and that one's beliefs in this area are reliable.

Justifications are *prima facie* or defeasible. The foundations theory allows, indeed insists, that one can be justified in believing something P and then come to believe something else that undermines one's justification for believing P. In that case one should stop believing P, unless one has some further justification that is not undermined.

I say "unless one has some further justification," because in this view a belief can have more than one justification. To be justified, a belief must have *at least* one justification. That is, if a belief in P is to be justified, it is required either that P be a foundational belief whose intrinsic justification is not defeated or that there be at least one undefeated justification of P from other beliefs one is justified in believing. If one believes P and it happens that all one's justifications for believing P come to be defeated, one is no longer justified in continuing to believe P, and one should subtract P from one's beliefs.

Furthermore, and this is important, if one comes not to be justified in continuing to believe P in this way, then not only is it true that one must abandon belief in P but justifications one has for other beliefs are also affected if these justifications appeal to one's belief in P. Justifications appealing to P must be abandoned when P is abandoned. If that means further beliefs are left without justification, then these beliefs too must be dropped along with any justifications appealing to them. So there will be a chain reaction when one loses justification for a belief on which other beliefs depend for their justification. (This is worked out in more detail for an artificial intelligence system by Doyle (1979, 1980).)

Now, it is an important aspect of the foundations theory of reasoning that justifications cannot legitimately be circular. P cannot be part of the justification for Q while Q is part of the justification for P (unless one of these beliefs has a different justification that does not appeal to the other belief).

The foundations theory also disallows infinite justifications. It does not allow P to be justified by appeal to Q, which is justified by appeal to R, and so on forever. Since justification cannot be circular, justification must eventually end in beliefs that either need no justification or are justified but not by appeal to other beliefs. Let us say that such basic or foundational beliefs are intrinsically justified.

For my purposes it does not matter exactly which beliefs are taken to be intrinsically justified in this sense. Furthermore, I emphasize that the foundations theory allows for situations in which a basic belief has its intrinsic justification defeated by one or more other beliefs, just as it allows for situations in which the justification of one belief in terms of other beliefs is defeated by still other beliefs. As I am interpreting it, foundationalism is not committed to the *incorrigibility* of basic beliefs.

A belief is a basic belief if it has an intrinsic justification which does not appeal to other beliefs. A basic belief can also have one or more nonintrinsic justifications which do appeal to other beliefs. So, a basic belief can have its intrinsic justification defeated and still remain justified as long as it retains at least one justification that is not defeated.

The existence of basic beliefs follows from the restrictions against circular and infinite justifications. Infinite justifications are to be ruled out because a finite creature can have only a finite number of beliefs, or at least only a finite number of *explicit beliefs*, whose content is explicitly represented in the brain. What one is justified in believing either implicitly or explicitly depends entirely one what one is justified in believing explicitly. To consider whether one's implicit beliefs are justified is to consider whether one is justified in believing the explicit beliefs on which the implicit beliefs depend. A justification for a belief that appeals to other beliefs must always appeal to things one believes explicitly. Since one has only finitely many explicit beliefs, there are only finitely many beliefs that can be appealed to for purposes of justification, and so infinite justifications are ruled out.

The Coherence Theory of Belief Revision

The coherence theory is *conservative* in a way the foundations theory is not. The coherence theory supposes one's present beliefs are justified just as they are in the absence of special reasons to change them, where changes are allowed only to the extent that they yield sufficient increases in coherence. This is a striking difference from the foundations theory. The foundations theory says one is justified in continuing to believe something only if one has a special reason to continue to accept that belief, whereas the coherence theory says one is justified in continuing to believe something as long as one has no special reason to stop believing it.

According to the coherence theory, if one's beliefs are incoherent in some way, because of outright inconsistency or simple *ad hoc*ness, then one should try to make minimal changes in those beliefs in order to eliminate the incoherence. More generally, small changes in one's beliefs are justified to the extent these changes add to the coherence of one's beliefs.

For present purposes, I do not need to be too specific as to exactly what coherence involves, except to say it includes not only consistency but also a network of relations among one's beliefs, especially relations of implication and explanation.

It is important that coherence competes with conservatism. It is as if there were two aims or tendencies of reasoned revision, to maximize coherence and to minimize change. Both tendencies are important. Without conservatism a person would be led to reduce his or her beliefs to the single Parmenidean thought that all is one. Without the tendency toward coherence we would have what Peirce (1877) called the method of tenacity, in which one holds to one's initial convictions no matter what evidence may accumulate against them.

According to the coherence theory, the assessment of a challenged belief is always holistic. Whether such a belief is justified depends on how well it fits together with everything else one believes. If one's beliefs are coherent, they are mutually supporting. All one's beliefs are, in a sense, equally fundamental. In the coherence theory there are not the asymmetrical justification relations among one's ongoing beliefs that there are in the foundations theory. It can happen in the coherence theory that P is justified because of the way it coheres with Q and Q is justified because of the way it coheres with P. In the foundations theory, such a pattern of justification is ruled out by the restriction against circular justification. But there is nothing wrong with circular justification in the coherence theory, especially if the circle is a large one!

I turn now to testing the foundations and coherence theories against our intuitions about cases. This raises an apparent problem for the coherence theory.

An Objection to the Coherence Theory: Karen's Aptitude Test

Sometimes there clearly are asymmetrical justification relations among one's beliefs.

Consider Karen, who has taken an aptitude test and has just been told her results show she has a considerable aptitude for science and music but little aptitude for history and philosophy. This news does not correlate perfectly with her previous grades. She had previously done well not only in physics, for which her aptitude scores are reported to be high, but also in history, for which her aptitude scores are reported to be low. Furthermore, she had previously done poorly not only in philosophy, for which her aptitude scores are reported to be low, but also in music, for which her aptitude scores are reported to be high.

After carefully thinking over these discrepancies, Karen concludes that her reported aptitude scores accurately reflect and are explained by her actual aptitudes; so she has an aptitude for science and music and no aptitude for history and philosophy; therefore her history course must have been an easy one, and also she did not work hard enough in the music course. She decides to take another music course and not to take any more history.

It seems quite clear that, in reaching these conclusions, Karen bases some of her beliefs on others. Her belief that the history course was easy depends for its justification on her belief that she has no aptitude for history, a belief which depends in turn for its justification on her belief that she got a low score in history on her aptitude test. There is no dependence in the other direction. For example, her belief about her aptitude test score in history is not based on her belief that she has no aptitude for history or on her belief that the history course was an easy one.

According to the coherence theory, the relevant relations here are merely *temporal* or *causal* relations. The coherence theory can agree that Karen's belief about the outcome of her aptitude test precedes and is an important cause of her belief that the history course she took was an easy one. But the coherence theory denies that a relation of dependence or justification holds or ought to hold between these two beliefs as time goes by, once the new belief has been firmly accepted.

In order to test this, let me tell more of Karen's story. Some days later she is informed that the report about her aptitude scores was incorrect! The scores reported were those of someone else whose name was confused with hers. Unfortunately, her own scores have now been lost. How should Karen revise her views, given this new information?

The foundations theory says she should abandon all beliefs whose justifications depend in part on her prior belief about her aptitude test scores. The only exception is for beliefs for which she can now find another and independent justification which does not depend on her belief about her aptitude test scores. She should continue to believe only those things she would have been justified in believing if she had never been given the false information about those scores. The foundations theory says this because it does not accept a principle of conservatism. The foundations theory does not allow that a belief can acquire justification simply by being believed.

Let us assume that, if Karen had not been given the false information about her aptitude test scores, she could not have reasonably reached any of the conclusions she did reach about her aptitudes for physics, history, philosophy, and music; and let us also assume that without those beliefs Karen could not have reached any of her further conclusions about the courses she has already taken. Then, according to the foundations theory, Karen should abandon her beliefs about her relative aptitudes for these subjects, and she should give up her belief that the history course she took was easy as well as her belief that she did not work hard enough in the music course. She should also reconsider her decisions to take another course in music and not to take any more history courses.

The coherence theory does not automatically yield the same advice that the foundations theory gives about this case. Karen's new information does produce a loss of overall coherence in her beliefs, since she can no longer coherently suppose that her aptitudes for science, music, philosophy, and history are in any way responsible for the original report she received about the results of her aptitude test. She must abandon that particular supposition about the explanation of the original report of her scores. Still, there is considerable coherence among the beliefs she inferred from this false report. For example, there is a connection between her belief that she has little aptitude for history, her belief that her high grade in the history course was the result of the course's being an easy one, and her belief that she will not take any more courses in history. There are similar connections between her beliefs about her aptitudes for other subjects, how well she did in courses in those subjects, and her plans for the future in those areas. Let us suppose that from the original report Karen inferred a great many other things that I haven't mentioned; so there are many beliefs involved here. Abandoning all these beliefs is costly from the point of view of conservatism, which says to minimize change. Suppose that there are so many of these beliefs and that they are so connected with each other and with other things Karen believes that the coherence theory implies Karen should retain all these new beliefs even though she must give up her beliefs about the explanation of the report of her aptitude scores. (In fact, we do not really need to suppose these beliefs are intricately connected with each other or even that there are many of them, since in the coherence theory a belief *does* acquire justification simply by being believed.)

The foundations theory says Karen should give up all these beliefs, whereas the coherence theory says Karen should retain them. Which theory is right about what Karen ought to do? Almost everyone who has considered this issue sides with the foundations theory: Karen should not retain any beliefs she inferred from the false report of her aptitude test scores that she would not have been justified in believing in the absence of that false report. That does seem to be the intuitively right answer. The foundations theory is in accordance with our intuitions about what Karen *ought* to do in a case like this. The coherence theory is not.

Belief Perseverance

In fact, Karen would almost certainly keep her new beliefs! That is what people actually do in situations like this. Although the foundations theory seems to give intuitively satisfying advice about what Karen *ought* to do in such a situation, the coherence theory is more in accord with what people actually do.

To document the rather surprising facts here, let me quote at some length from a recent survey article (Ross and Anderson 1982, pp. 147–149), which speaks of

> the dilemma of the social psychologist who has made use of deception in the course of an experiment and then seeks to debrief

the subjects who had been the target of such deception. The psychologist reveals the totally contrived and inauthentic nature of the information presented presuming that this debriefing will thereby eliminate any effects such information might have exerted upon the subjects' feelings or beliefs. Many professionals, however, have expressed public concern that such experimental deception may do great harm that is not fully undone by conventional debriefing procedures. . . .

Ross and Anderson go on to describe experiments designed to "explore" what they call "the phenomenon of belief perseverance in the face of evidential discrediting." In one experiment,

Subjects first received continuous false feedback as they performed a novel discrimination task (i.e., distinguishing authentic suicide notes from fictitious ones). . . . [Then each subject] received a standard debriefing session in which he learned that his putative outcome had been predetermined and that his feedback had been totally unrelated to actual performance. . . . [E]very subject was led to explicitly acknowledge his understanding of the nature and purpose of the experimental deception.

Following this total discrediting of the original information, the subjects completed a dependent variable questionnaire dealing with [their] performance and abilities. The evidence for postdebriefing impression perseverance was unmistakable. . . . On virtually every measure . . . the totally discredited initial outcome manipulation produced significant "residual" effects upon [subjects'] . . . assessments. . . .

Follow-up experiments have since shown that a variety of unfounded personal impressions, once induced by experimental procedures, can survive a variety of total discrediting procedures. For example, Jennings, Lepper, and Ross . . . have demonstrated that subjects' impressions of their ability at interpersonal persuasion (having them succeed or fail to convince a confederate to donate blood) can persist after they have learned that the initial outcome was totally inauthentic. Similarly, . . . two related experiments have shown that students' erroneous impressions of their "logical problem solving abilities" (and their academic choices in a follow-up measure two months later) persevered even after they had learned that good or poor teaching procedures provided a totally sufficient explanation for the successes or failures that were the basis for such impressions.

... [Other] studies first manipulated and then attempted to undermine subjects' theories about the functional relationship between two measured variables: the adequacy of firefighters' professional performances and their prior scores on a paper and pencil test of risk performance. . . . [S]uch theories survived the revelations that the cases in question had been totally fictitious and the different subjects had, in fact, received opposite pairings of riskiness scores and job outcomes. . . . [O]ver 50% of the initial effect of the "case history" information remained after debriefing.

In summary, it is clear that beliefs can survive . . . the total destruction of their original evidential bases.

It is therefore quite likely that Karen will continue to believe many of the things she inferred from the false report of her aptitude test scores. She will continue to believe these things even after learning that the report was false.

The Habit Theory of Belief

Why is it so hard for subjects to be debriefed? Why do people retain conclusions they have drawn from evidence that is now discredited? One possibility is that belief is a kind of habit. This is an implication of behaviorism, the view that beliefs and other mental attitudes are habits of behavior. But the suggestion that beliefs are habits might be correct even apart from behaviorism. The relevant habits need not be overt behavioral habits. They might be habits of thought. Perhaps, to believe that *P* is to be disposed to *think* that *P* under certain conditions, to be disposed to use this thought as a premise or assumption in reasoning and in deciding what to do. Then, once a belief has become established, considerable effort might be needed to get rid of it, even if the believer should come to see that he or she ought to get rid of it, just as it is hard to get rid of other bad habits. One can't simply decide to get rid of a bad habit; one must take active steps to ensure that the habit does not reassert itself. Perhaps it is just as difficult to get rid of a bad belief.

Goldman (1978) mentions a related possibility, observing that Anderson and Bower (1973) treat coming to believe something as the establishing of connections, or "associative links," between relevant conceptual representations in the brain. Now, it may be that, once set up, such connections or links cannot easily be broken unless competing connections are set up that overwhelm the original ones. The easiest case might be that in which one starts by believing *P* and then comes to believe *not P* by setting up stronger connections involving *not P* than those involved in believing *P*. It might be much harder simply to give up one's belief in *P* without substituting a contrary belief. According to this model of belief, in order to stop believing *P*, it would not be enough simply to notice passively that one's evidence for *P* had been discredited. One would have to take positive steps to counteract the associations that constitute one's belief in *P*. The difficulties in giving up a discredited belief would be similar in this view to the difficulties envisioned in the habit theory of belief.

But this explanation does not give a plausible account of the phenomenon of belief perseverance. Of course, there are cases in which one has to struggle in order to abandon a belief one takes to be discredited. One finds oneself coming back to thoughts one realizes one should no longer accept. There are such habits of thought, but this is not what is happening in the debriefing studies. Subjects in these studies are not struggling to abandon beliefs they see are discredited. On the contrary, the subjects do not see that the beliefs they have acquired have been discredited. They come up with all sorts of "rationalizations" (as we say) appealing to connections with other beliefs of a sort that the coherence theory, but not the foundations theory, might approve. So the correct explanation of belief perseverance in these studies is not that beliefs which have lost their evidential grounding are like bad habits.

Positive versus Negative Undermining

In fact, what the debriefing studies show is that people simply do not keep track of the justification relations among their beliefs. They continue to believe things after the evidence for them has been discredited because they do not realize what they are doing. They do not understand that the discredited evidence was the *sole* reason why they believe as they do. They do not see they would not have been justified in forming those beliefs in the absence of the now discredited evidence. They do not realize these beliefs have been undermined. It is this, rather than the difficulty of giving up bad habits, that is responsible for belief perseverance.

The foundations theory says people should keep track of their reasons for believing as they do and should stop believing anything that is not associated with adequate evidence. So the foundations theory implies that, if Karen has not kept track of her reason for believing her history course was an easy one, she should have abandoned her belief even before she was told about the mix-up with her aptitude test scores. This seems clearly wrong.

Furthermore, since people rarely keep track of their reasons, the theory implies that people are unjustified in almost all their beliefs. This is an absurd result! The foundations theory turns out not to be a plausible normative theory after all. So let us see whether we cannot defend the coherence theory as a normative theory.

We have already seen how the coherence theory can appeal to a nonholistic *causal* notion of local justification by means of a limited number of one's prior beliefs, namely, those prior beliefs that are most crucial to one's justification for adding the new belief. The coherence theory does not suppose there are *continuing* links of justification dependency that can be consulted when revising one's beliefs. But the theory can admit that Karen's coming to believe certain things depended on certain of her prior beliefs in a way that it did not depend on others, where this dependence represents a kind of local justification, even though in another respect whether Karen was justified in coming to believe those things depended on everything she then believed.

Given this point, I suggest the coherence theory can suppose it is incoherent to believe both *P* and also that all one's reasons for believing *P* relied crucially on false assumptions. Within the coherence theory, this implies, roughly, the following:

> *Principle of Positive Undermining*   One should stop believing *P* whenever one positively believes one's reasons for believing *P* are no good.

This is only roughly right, since there is also the possibility that one should instead stop believing that one's reasons for *P* are no good, as well as the possibility that one cannot decide between that belief and *P*. In any event, I want to compare this rough statement of the principle with the corresponding principle in a foundations theory:

> *Principle of Negative Undermining*   One should stop believing *P* whenever one does not associate one's belief in *P* with an adequate justification (either intrinsic or extrinsic).

The Principle of Positive Undermining is much more plausible than the Principle of Negative Undermining. The Principle of Negative Undermining implies that, as one loses track of the justifications of one's beliefs, one should give up those beliefs. But, if one does not keep track of one's justifications for most of one's beliefs, as seems to be the case, then the Principle of Negative Undermining says that one should stop believing almost everything one believes, which is absurd. On the other hand the Principle of Positive Undermining does not have this absurd implication. The Principle of Positive Undermining does not suppose that the absence of a justification is a reason to stop believing something. It only supposes that one's belief in P is undermined by the *positive* belief that one's reasons for P are no good.

It is relevant that subjects *can* be successfully debriefed after experiments involving deception if they are made vividly aware of the phenomenon of belief perseverance, that is, if they are made vividly aware of the tendency for people to retain false beliefs after the evidence for them has been undercut, and if they are also made vividly aware of how this phenomenon has acted in their own case (Nisbett and Ross 1980, p. 177). It might be suggested that this shows that under ideal conditions people really do act in accordance with the foundations theory after all, so that the foundations theory *is* normatively correct as an account of how one ideally ought to revise one's beliefs. But in fact this further phenomenon seems clearly to support the coherence theory, with its Principle of Positive Undermining, and not the foundations theory, with its Principle of Negative Undermining. The so-called process debriefing cannot merely undermine the evidence for the conclusions subjects have reached but must also directly attack each of these conclusions themselves. Process debriefing works not just by getting subjects to give up beliefs that originally served as evidence for the conclusions they have reached but by getting them to accept certain further positive beliefs about their lack of good reasons for each of these conclusions.

What about Our Intuitions?

It may seem to fly in the face of common sense to suppose that the coherence theory is normatively correct in cases like this. Remember that, after carefully considering Karen's situation, almost everyone agrees she should give up all beliefs inferred from the original false report, except those beliefs which would have been justified apart from any appeal to evidence tainted by that false information. Almost everyone's judgment about what Karen ought to do coincides with what the foundations theory says she ought to do. Indeed, psychologists who have studied the phenomenon of belief perseverance in the face of debriefing consider it to be a paradigm of irrationality. How can these strong normative intuitions possibly be taken to be mistaken, as they must be if the coherence theory is to be accepted as normatively correct?

The answer is that, when people think about Karen's situation, they ignore the possibility that she may have failed to keep track of the justifications of her beliefs. They imagine Karen is or ought to be aware that she no longer has any good reasons for the beliefs she inferred from the false report. And, of course, this is to imagine that Karen is violating the Principle of Positive Undermining. It is hard to allow for the possibility that she may be violating not that principle but only the foundationalist's Principle of Negative Undermining.

Keeping Track of Justification

People do not seem to keep track of the justifications of their beliefs. If we try to suppose that people do keep track of their justifications, we would have to suppose that either they fail to notice when their justifications are undermined or they do notice but have great difficulty in abandoning the unjustified beliefs in the way a person has difficulty abandoning a bad habit. Neither possibility offers a plausible account of the phenomenon of belief perseverance.

It stretches credulity to suppose people always keep track of the sources of their beliefs but often fail to notice when these sources are undermined. That is like supposing people always remember everything that has ever happened to them but cannot always retrieve the stored information from memory. To say one remembers something is to say one has stored it in a way that normally allows it to be retrieved at will. Similarly, to say people keep track of the sources of their beliefs must be to say they can normally use this information when it is appropriate to do so.

I have already remarked that the other possibility seems equally incredible, namely, that people have trouble abandoning the undermined beliefs in the way they have trouble getting rid of bad habits. To repeat, participants in belief perseverance studies show no signs of knowing their beliefs are ungrounded. They do not act like people struggling with their beliefs as with bad habits. Again, I agree it sometimes happens that one keeps returning to thoughts after one has seen there can be no reason to accept those thoughts. There are habits of thought that can be hard to get rid of. But that is not what is going on in the cases psychologists study under the name of belief perseverance.

This leaves the issue of whether one should *try* always to keep track of the local justifications of one's beliefs, even if, in fact, people do not seem to do this. I want to consider the possibility that there is a good reason for not keeping track of these justifications.

Clutter Avoidance Again

We have seen there is a practical reason to avoid too much clutter in one's beliefs. There is a limit to what one can remember, a limit to the number of things one can put into long-term storage, and a limit to what one can retrieve. It is important to save room for important things and not clutter one's mind with a lot of unimportant matters. This is an important reason why one does not try to believe all sorts of logical consequences of one's beliefs. One should not try to infer all one can from one's beliefs. One should try not to retain too much trivial information. Furthermore, one should try to store in long-term memory only the key matters that one will later need to recall. When one reaches a significant conclusion from one's other beliefs, one needs to remember the conclusion but does not normally need to remember all the intermediate steps involved in reaching that conclusion. Indeed, one should not try to remember those intermediate steps; one should try to avoid too much clutter in one's mind.

Similarly, even if much of one's knowledge of the world is inferred ultimately from what one believes oneself to be immediately perceiving at one or another time, one does not normally need to remember these original perceptual beliefs or many of the various intermediate conclusions drawn from them. It is enough to recall the more important of one's conclusions. This means one should not be disposed to try to keep track of the local justifications of one's beliefs. One could keep track of these justifications only by remembering an incredible number of mostly perceptual original premises, along with many, many intermediate steps which one does not want and has little need to remember. One will not want to link one's beliefs to such justifications because one will not in general want to try to retain the prior beliefs from which one reached one's current beliefs.

The practical reason for not keeping track of the justifications of one's beliefs is not as severe as the reason that prevents one from trying to operate purely probabilistically, using generalized conditionalization as one's only principle of reasoned revision. The problem is not that there would be a combinatorial explosion. Still, there are important practical constraints. It is more efficient not to try to retain these justifications and the accompanying justifying beliefs. This leaves more room in memory for important matters.

Chapter 5

Implicit Commitments

More on Positive Undermining

In chapter 4 I stated the Principle of Positive Undermining somewhat roughly: "One should stop believing *P* whenever one positively believes one's reasons for believing *P* are no good." Let us now try to be more specific about the content of the undermining belief that one's reasons are "no good."

One suggestion would be that the relevant undermining belief is simply the belief that one is not now justified in believing *P*. But this cannot be right. Sometimes, thinking one's reasons for believing *P* are "no good" in the relevant sense, one follows the Principle of Positive Undermining and concludes that one is not justified in believing *P*. In such a case one's belief that one's reasons are "no good" has to be different from the belief that one is "not justified." Otherwise, one could not get started. One could not reach the conclusion that one's belief in *P* is unjustified without first having already reached that conclusion!

This may suggest the relevant belief is that one's reasons are "no good" in the sense that one was not *originally* justified in believing *P* when one first formed that belief. One could first believe *that* and then use the Principle of Positive Undermining to conclude that one is still not justified in believing *P*. But this is not right either. Karen was originally justified in reaching the various conclusions she reached on the basis of the initial report about her aptitude test scores. Later, given a full process debriefing that makes her vividly aware of what has happened in her case, she may come to see that her reasons are "no good," but that is not the same as coming to see she was originally unjustified, since she was justified originally.

At one point in chapter 4 I stated the general principle like this: "It is incoherent to believe both *P* and also that all one's reasons for believing *P* relied crucially on false assumptions." This accounts for Karen's situation after a process debriefing. At that point she realizes she had been justified in accepting various conclusions only because of her belief in the accuracy of the original report of her aptitude test scores, a belief that she now sees is false.

I think this covers all the relevant cases. Although there may seem to be cases in which one comes to think one's original reasons are "no good," where this does not involve having relied on false beliefs, in all such cases I think there is a relevant *implicit* false belief.

Reliability Commitment

Consider this example. William looks out the window and, on the basis of what he sees, forms the belief that the girl his daughter is playing with in the backyard is the girl he met yesterday, named Connie. Later he learns Connie has an identical twin, Laura, whom he cannot distinguish from Connie. This leads him to realize that his reasons for his belief about the identity of the girl he saw playing with his daughter in the backyard are "no good." The Principle of Positive Undermining should apply here. It may seem that, in applying this Principle, William does not have to suppose that his original justification relied on any false beliefs. In particular, he needn't have explicitly considered whether Connie might have an identical twin.

But in such a case William at least implicitly relied on the belief that the perceptual appearances were an objectively reliable indicator of the identity of the girl he saw with his daughter. On learning that Connie has an identical twin, he now thinks appearances were not an objectively reliable indicator, so he thinks he was (subjectively) justified only because he relied on a false belief. The relevant belief here, that the appearances are an objectively reliable indicator, is, to repeat, ordinarily implicit rather than explicit. It is something William is committed to in coming to believe that the girl he sees is the same girl as the one he spoke to earlier, whether or not he explicitly notes this commitment.

Karen has a similar implicit belief. When she reaches her conclusions about her aptitudes and related matters, she assumes, at least implicitly, that the reports of her scores are an objectively reliable indicator of her scores. More generally, whenever one infers something new, one supposes one's grounds are an objectively reliable indicator of the truth of one's conclusion.

The existence of such commitments helps to account for a tendency some people have to think S does not know that P even if it is true that P and S is justified in believing that P, if S's grounds are not a reliable indicator of the truth of S's conclusion (Goldman 1976). For we might refuse to credit S with knowing that P if S's belief that P involves a commitment that is false (Harman 1980).

Likelihood

Objective reliability is a kind of objective likelihood or probability. To say that evidence is a reliable indicator of a conclusion on a particular occasion is to say that on that occasion, given the evidence, there is no significant likelihood that the conclusion is false.

The following example indicates how objective likelihood can differ from "epistemic" likelihood. Suppose George has a bag of marbles, some red, some white, and George randomly selects a marble from the bag. It may be that, although George does not know this, a quarter of the marbles are white, the rest red. Then the objective likelihood that the marble George selects is white is 1/4, whereas the epistemic likelihood may be 1/2 (if it has any definite value at all).

Similarly, William's reasons for believing Connie is in the backyard are "no good" because, given his reasons, here is a significant objective likelihood that his belief is false, even if there is no significant epistemic likelihood of this for him until he learns about Connie's sister.

Objective likelihood is a relative notion. Something can be likely in relation to certain facts and unlikely in relation to others. There is a significant likelihood that a girl William takes to be Connie is really her sister, Laura. There is no significant likelihood that a girl whom William takes to be Connie and who parts her hair in the middle of her head is Laura, since Laura always parts her hair on the left. In other words, in relation to the fact that William takes it to be Connie in the backyard, there is a significant likelihood that it is not Connie; but, in relation to the fact that William takes her to be Connie and she parts her pair in the middle, there is no significant likelihood that it is not Connie.

Now, notice that William's reasons for believing that it is Connie in the backyard might well mention incidently that the girl in the backyard parts her hair in the middle. Then there is no significant likelihood that his belief is false, given a full statement of reasons. But his reasons are still "no good," since he does not know this distinguishes Connie from Laura.

Later, after William becomes familiar with the two twins, he might come to believe he is seeing Connie in the backyard on the basis of a similar presentation, again noticing the fact that her hair is parted in the middle. At this point his reasons are not "no good," since he now knows that this is what distinguishes Connie from Laura.

At first, William assumes that a certain general appearance is a reliable indicator of Connie's presence. Later he does not assume this and assumes only that such an appearance including hair parted in the middle is a reliable indicator of Connie's presence. This shows that the precise assumptions one makes about reliability depend on one's actual reasoning.

Conservatism: Tentative versus Full Acceptance

In chapter 4 I argued that beliefs and intentions are subject to the following:

> *Principle of Conservatism*   One is justified in continuing fully to accept something in the absence of a special reason not to.

The Principle applies to what one fully accepts, what one fully believes or fully intends. It does not apply to the things one accepts as working hypotheses or tentative plans. In order to help bring out some of the force of this Principle, I now want to contrast these two sorts of acceptance, full acceptance and the more tentative acceptance of something as a working hypothesis. (I will discuss accepting something as a working hypothesis and will not say anything explicitly about accepting something as a working plan, although much that is true of working hypotheses is also true of working plans.)

To accept something as a working hypothesis is to "try it out," to see where one gets by accepting it, to see what further things such acceptance leads to. Accepting a particular working hypothesis is fruitful if it allows one to make sense of various phenomena; if it leads to solutions of problems, particularly when there are independent checks on these solutions; and if it leads naturally to other similarly fruitful hypotheses.

If a working hypothesis is sufficiently fruitful, one may become justified in fully accepting it. One's reason for such full acceptance or belief will not be the same as one's reason for having first accepted the hypothesis as a working hypothesis. One's original reason for having tentatively accepted a working hypothesis was that such acceptance promised to be fruitful. One's later reason for coming fully to accept or believe the hypothesis is that it has indeed proved fruitful in a way that suggests it is true.

This is not to say there is a sharp line between full beliefs and working hypotheses. One's acceptance of a working hypothesis can gradually become more than tentative, so that eventually one is no longer investigating that hypothesis but has fully accepted it. Things can go the other way, too. If "anomalies" arise with respect to a view, one can pass from fully accepting it to accepting it more tentatively and merely as a working hypothesis.

One is justified in continuing to accept something as a working hypothesis only as long as such acceptance promises to pay off. If something has been tentatively accepted already for some time, one is normally justified in continuing one's tentative acceptance of it only if such acceptance has already proved fruitful. It is not enough merely to be able to rebut objections in the sense that one can develop auxiliary hypotheses that keep one from being refuted. One also needs a positive payoff. One should avoid "degenerating research programs" (Lakatos 1970).

The Principle of Conservatism does not apply to such tentative acceptance. It is not true that one is justified in continuing to accept a working hypothesis in the absence of a special reason not to. One needs a special positive reason to keep on accepting something as a working hypothesis. (However, a looser strategic principle may be relevant. Perhaps, one should not too quickly abandon what one tentatively accepts simply because there is no immediate payoff. One should not get discouraged too quickly.)

Tentative acceptance is not easy. It takes a certain amount of sophistication and practice to be able to investigate an issue by tentatively accepting various hypotheses. Ordinary people, and even most scientists, are quick to convert tentative acceptance to full acceptance in a way that seems overly hasty to critical reflection (Nisbett and Ross 1980, chap. 8).

Full Acceptance Ends Inquiry

Belief in or full acceptance of P involves two things. First, one allows oneself to use P as part of one's starting point in further theoretical and practical thinking. Second, one takes the issue to be closed in the sense that, when one fully accepts P, one is no longer investigating whether P is true. Granted, one may continue investigating in order to get evidence that will stand up in court or for some other reason, but one is no longer investigating in order to find out whether P is true. In fully accepting P, one takes oneself to *know* that P is true.

Accepting something as a working hypothesis has the first of these features. If one accepts something as a working hypothesis, one can then use it as part of one's starting point in further thinking. But this sort of acceptance does not have the second feature. In accepting something as a working hypothesis, one is not ending inquiry into that matter. On the contrary, one is pursuing the inquiry in a particular way.

Since full acceptance does end inquiry in this way, one is *justified* in fully accepting P only if one is justified in ending one's investigation into whether P is true. This means one has to be justified in implicitly supposing that further investigation would not be sufficiently worthwhile, for example, by uncovering relevant evidence of a sort not yet considered. Popper (1959) stresses the point: It is not enough to look for positive evidence in favor of a hypothesis; one must also try to find evidence against the hypothesis. A hypothesis is "corroborated" only to the extent that it survives one's best attempts to refute it. Only then can one suppose further investigation would not be worthwhile. That is why it is important to check a variety of instances before accepting a generalization; it is not enough that one has checked many instances and found they are in accordance with the generalization if all the instances checked are of the same sort and if there are other sorts one has not checked (Hempel 1966).

Popper also argues against fully accepting any scientific hypothesis, but we can appreciate his methodological point without agreeing with that. Perhaps Popper believes with Malcolm (1963) and Unger (1975) that full acceptance can only end inquiry if it involves a dogmatic commitment to disregard future negative evidence. But that is not true. Having ended inquiry at one time, one may always reopen it later. The point is merely that a special reason is needed to justify reopening an inquiry. The Principle of Conservatism applies.

Full acceptance ends inquiry into P in the sense that, having accepted P, one is justified in continuing to accept P in the absence of a special reason to doubt P or at least a special reason to reopen one's inquiry. Having accepted P, one is no longer actively looking for evidence as to whether P is true. One will now pass up opportunities to find such evidence, opportunities one would be pursuing if one had not ended one's investigation into P.

To take a trivial example, suppose Mark is trying to discover how to get to an address on a street called Prospect Place. Mark's "investigation" consists in asking a passerby if he knows how to get there. If the passerby is sufficiently hesitant, Mark can check the directions by asking others. (Mark may even think it prudent to ask a second person even if the first seemed quite confident.) But once Mark comes fully to accept an answer, Mark's "investigation" is over. Mark will not at that point continue to ask others how to get to Prospect Place. (At least, Mark will not do so in order to find out how to get there. He might continue asking others for some other reason, for example, to see how many people know where Prospect Place is, to hear the local accent, or whatever.)

Full acceptance of P may therefore involve an implicit commitment to the claim that further investigation of P would not be worthwhile, for example, in leading one to discover further evidence that would lead to a reassessment of one's conclusion. This might explain the following otherwise puzzling aspect of some people's judgments about knowledge. Many people are reluctant to say someone knows a certain conclusion if there is easily available evidence that (misleadingly, as it happens) casts doubt on the truth of that conclusion, for example a forged document on the person's desk that he or she has not yet seen. Perhaps this reluctance to allow the person knows is based on the falsity of something the person is committed to in fully accepting that conclusion, namely that there is no easily available evidence that should lead to such a reassessment (Harman 1980).

Why Full Acceptance?

I have already observed that people find it difficult to accept things only tentatively as mere working hypotheses. There is a strong tendency quickly to convert such tentative acceptance into full acceptance. Why is this so? Why can't we always accept things tentatively as working hypotheses and refrain from ever fully believing anything?

At least part of the answer is that something like the foundations theory applies to what one tentatively accepts as a working hypothesis, as part of one's investigation of something. The same practical limits that keep one from operating in accordance with the foundations theory also keep one from never ending inquiry and always tentatively accepting one's conclusions as mere working hypotheses.

In the midst of inquiry one needs to keep track of which tentatively accepted things depend on others, so that ongoing revisions can be neatly accommodated. One needs to remember what reasons there are for and against various possible outcomes of the inquiry, where this can involve also the reasons for various possible intermediate conclusions.

Consider the situation of jurors at a trial. The jurors first hear one side of the case then the other. They are not supposed to reach firm conclusions about any aspect of the case until all the evidence is in and both sides have had their say. At that point, the jurors are supposed to take all the evidence into account in reaching their own conclusions. This often involves keeping track of a number of different considerations, replies, rebuttals, and so on. It is important that the juror try to remember all the relevant evidence and arguments and the various ways these relate to each other. It would not be good for the jurors to listen to one side and reach various provisional conclusions without remembering the reasons for these conclusions. If the jurors were to forget these reasons, how would they be able to give a fair assessment of the other side of the case?

Even after the individual jurors reach their own conclusions, they must still try to keep track of all the evidence until the jury as a whole reaches a verdict. After that, it is no longer necessary to remember the reasons for the verdict, since the inquiry is now closed.

Ordinary inquiry shares features with the jurors' predicament. Until an inquiry is ended, one needs to keep a record of reasons for various conclusions, possible counters to these reasons, counters to those counters, and so on. This means one must keep track of dependencies among one's tentative hypotheses. If one had unlimited powers of record keeping and an unlimited ability to survey ever more complex structures of argument, replies, rebuttals, and so on, it would be rational always to accept things only tentatively as working hypotheses, never ending inquiry. But since one does not have such unlimited powers of record keeping and has a quite limited ability to survey reasons and arguments, one is forced to limit the amount of inquiry in which one is engaged and one must fully accept most of the conclusions one accepts, thereby ending inquiry. Tentative acceptance must remain a special case of acceptance. It cannot be the general rule.

Acceptance for Oneself and for Others

One accepts things in different ways. In addition to the distinction between fully accepting or believing something and accepting it merely as a working hypothesis, there is also a distinction between accepting something only for oneself and accepting it as a member of a group.

Clearly, one often accepts propositions on the authority of others. One takes someone's word for it—a teacher, an authority, a passerby who claims to know where Prospect Place is. Furthermore, one is often willing to make authoritative statements oneself, for others to rely on. One tells things to one's children or one's students, one gives directions, and so on (Austin 1946). But one is not always willing to do this. Sometimes one is reluctant to give advice to others. Sometimes one is willing to say such things as, "Albert is in his office. You can take my word for it; I guarantee it." But at other times one is willing to say only something much weaker, "Albert is in his office; that's what I believe anyway," or "For myself I am certain that Albert is in his office, but see for yourself; don't take my word for it."

When one asks others whether they are *sure* or whether they *know*, one is often asking whether they guarantee it in this sense. One is not normally just asking about their subjective certainty or whether they think they know. It makes sense to say, "I think I know, but see for yourself."

One is subject to blame if one guarantees something that turns out not to be so. This goes beyond being subject to criticism for any *individual* failing. Compare the difference between, "My present intention is to be at the party" and "I promise that I will be at the party." If one merely states one's intention, one might be criticized for having formed an intention one shouldn't have formed; but, if one was fully justified in forming that intention, one would not be criticized for having later changed one's mind, given a new situation. But, if one promised, one can also be criticized for not being at the party, where this goes beyond any criticism one might receive for one's original intention or promise. So, promising involves an additional commitment that one does not have when one simply announces an intention. When one guarantees that something is so, one in a sense promises that others may rely on the truth of what one says, in a way that no such promise is involved in simply expressing one's opinions. An authoritative statement involves an additional responsibility. One might be blamed for guaranteeing that something is so which is not so, where this goes beyond any criticism one might receive for having expressed an unjustified opinion on the subject.

The use of authority in this way is important. It promotes the growth of human knowledge. Each person does not have to start all over again from scratch. Appeal to authority also plays a role in learning new terminology, since one must often accept certain principles, at least as assumptions or working hypotheses, before one can use the terminology in a way that constitutes mastery of the terminology.

Now, I suggest that the distinction between expressions of merely personal opinion and authoritative statements reflects a difference in ways in which things are accepted. Sometimes one accepts something merely for oneself and sometimes one accepts something on behalf of or as something acceptable to a group. The clearest cases of this occur in inquiries that are explicitly group endeavors, involving teams of detectives or scientists. Individual members of such groups sometimes reach conclusions as members of the group or *for* the group, and special constraints apply to such acceptance. In particular, a member of such a group should not accept something in an authoritative way for the group as a conclusion of the group unless he or she can coherently suppose there is no relevant evidence he or she hasn't considered that is possessed by others in the group.

I suggest that such group inquiry is in fact the usual case. Learning about the world is a cooperative enterprise. One comes to accept things as a member of one's family or society or profession or culture. It is only when people become methodologically self-conscious that they distinguish their own private opinions from the things they accept as members of a group.

This may explain why we are sometimes reluctant to say someone knows something, even if he or she believes it for the right reason, if there is misleading undermining evidence which most people know about of which the person in question is unaware. To take an example from Harman (1973), suppose a political leader is assassinated in full view of the press. The *New York Times* publishes a detailed account in its early edition. However, officials deny that the person killed is the political leader in question. They say it was someone else. Suppose these (lying) denials are widely heard and given some credence. Alice wakes up, goes to her front door, and brings in the *New York Times* to read at breakfast. She receives the early edition, printed before the official denials. Reading the (accurate) story about the assassination, she comes to believe that the political leader in question has been killed. She believes something that is true, she is justified in believing it, and her reasons are the right reasons. But does she know that the political leader has been assassinated? People do not agree about what to say about this, but many are reluctant to say she knows, although they think she would know if it were not for the official denials. It may be that the reason for their reluctance is this. In accepting a claim as something one knows, one accepts it as a member of some relevant group, and so one is committed to the claim that one's evidential position is not undermined by evidence possessed by others in the group. Since that commitment is wrong in this case, Alice does not know.

Conclusion

I have discussed four sorts of commitment involved in the usual case of fully believing P in an authoritative way. First, in fully believing P one is committed to the claim that one has or had sufficient reasons for believing P that did not rely on any false assumptions. Second, when one infers that something is so, one is committed to a claim that there is no significant chance that one's conclusion is false, given one's reasons for it (where the exact claim to which one is committed depends on the details of one's reasoning). Third, in ending inquiry into P, one is committed to the claim that further inquiry into P should not affect one's conclusion. Fourth, in accepting P as a member of a particular group, one is committed to the claim that evidence that should affect one's conclusions is not possessed by others in one's group.

These commitments reflect different aspects of inquiry. The first reflects the way beliefs may be given up via the Principle of Positive Undermining. The second reflects the way inquiry is sensitive to objective likelihoods. The third reflects the fact that full belief ends inquiry. And the fourth reflects the social character of most inquiry.

Commitments of the first three sorts are harder to escape than commitments of the last sort. Because of one's finite and limited powers, one cannot escape the first three commitments except in a few instances when one is able tentatively to accept certain propositions merely as working hypotheses. One can handle only a limited amount of such tentative acceptance since one can engage in only a limited amount of inquiry at any one time. But it may be possible to escape the fourth commitment by refusing to accept things as a member of a group and accept things only for oneself. That may not be fair, but the constraint here seems to be more a matter of morality than a result of limited personal powers, in the way the first two commitments depend on one's limited powers. True, one could hardly survive in the modern world without making use of the outcomes of group inquiry; but that is not to say one must oneself now participate in order to survive.

Chapter 6

Some Principles of Belief Revision

The Relevance of Interests

We have seen that, because of the limitations of finiteness, one is subject to a principle of

> *Clutter Avoidance*   One should not clutter one's mind with trivialities.

Since trivialities, in the relevant sense, are matters in which one has no interest, this suggests the following policy:

> *Interest Condition (on theoretical reasoning)*   One is to add a new proposition *P* to one's beliefs only if one is interested in whether *P* is true (and it is otherwise reasonable for one to believe *P*).

The interest need not be a strong one; it could be a trivial whim. But, according to the Interest Condition, there must be some such interest if one is to be warranted in coming to accept a new belief.

One's interest in whether *P* is true may be simple, unmotivated curiosity, but it will more often arise in accordance with such principles as the following:

> *Interest in the Environment*   One has a reason to be interested in objects and events in one's immediate environment. (So one fairly automatically notices "salient occurrences" that are "right before one's eyes.")
>
> *Interest in Facilitating Practical Reasoning*   If one desires *E* and believes *M*'s being true would facilitate or hinder *E*, one has a reason to be interested in whether *M* is true.
>
> *Interest in Facilitating Theoretical Reasoning*   If one is interested in whether *P* is true and has reason to believe knowing whether *Q* is true would facilitate knowing whether *P* is true, one has a reason to be interested in whether *Q* is true.

Notice that there is an important respect in which one can be interested in whether *Q* is true without being interested in whether *not Q* is true.

Suppose one is interested in whether P is true and suppose Q obviously implies P. Then one may be interested in whether Q is true, because if one knew Q was true, one could conclude that P was true. So, given strong evidence for Q, one ·has reason to accept it. But given strong evidence for *not Q*, one may fail to have any reason to accept *not Q*, since accepting *not Q* need not help one to reach a conclusion about whether P is true.

Granted, acceptance of *not Q* might be useful in keeping one from later trying that possibility again; it might keep one from later repeating one's work by trying again to see whether Q is true. It is useful to have some record of ways one knows one cannot get to P. But this does not normally mean one will want to keep an explicit record of *all* failed attempts. It is enough to note general characteristics of unsuccessful routes.

This is not an endorsement of wishful thinking. In particular, it is not to suggest that, if there is roughly the same evidence for and against P, then whether one should conclude P or *not P* depends on what one is interested in. In such a case, one should not reach either conclusion, no matter what one's interests. (At least this is true of theoretical reasoning, the conclusions of which are beliefs. On the other hand wishful thinking of a certain sort is quite permissible in practical reasoning, since a decision between intending P and intending *not P* can quite properly depend on which of these one prefers.) The point is rather that, even if the evidence for P is overwhelming, one should not add P to one's beliefs unless one is interested in whether P is true.

The Interest in Not Being Inconsistent

Whether and how one will change one's view depends to some extent on one's interests. But one cannot just ignore inconsistencies in one's view on the grounds that one does not happen to be interested in them. One always has a reason to be interested in avoiding inconsistency. This is reflected in the strong tendency one has to avoid inconsistency.

Actually one has two tendencies: (1) a tendency to avoid holding beliefs that are immediately inconsistent, and (2) a tendency to avoid holding beliefs that one recognizes to be indirectly or less obviously inconsistent. Beliefs are indirectly inconsistent if there is a possible argument each step of which represents an immediate implication from those beliefs to conclusions that leave one's beliefs immediately inconsistent.

Tendency (2) is needed. Otherwise, when faced with an obvious inconsistency, one could simply abandon one of the explicitly competing beliefs without giving up any of the beliefs that imply it. Tendency (1) is part of what it is for beliefs to be immediately inconsistent. Tendency (2) depends on having an ability to recognize indirect implications, which in turn depends on one's being disposed to take certain propositions immediately to imply others. (Immediate implications therefore play a role not only in accepting new beliefs implied by old beliefs but also in avoiding indirect inconsistency.)

Both tendencies depend on one's having recognized that one's beliefs are either immediately or indirectly inconsistent. But recognizing an immediate inconsistency is importantly different from recognizing an indirect inconsistency. Recognizing that certain beliefs are immediately inconsistent is directly manifested in the tendency to treat beliefs of that sort as inconsistent; one is not propelled by a separate belief that the original beliefs are inconsistent. But one's recognition that one's beliefs are indirectly inconsistent cannot be directly manifested in a tendency to treat beliefs of that sort as inconsistent, because then those beliefs would be immediately inconsistent, not just indirectly inconsistent. So, one's tendency to avoid indirect inconsistency does depend on an explicit belief that some of one's other beliefs are inconsistent.

This suggests that tendency (2) can be expressed as (2a) a tendency to avoid holding beliefs which include the belief that some of one's other beliefs are jointly inconsistent. We can account for (2a) in terms of more basic principles. To believe that $P, \ldots, R$ are inconsistent is to believe that $P, \ldots, R$ imply something, A, that is immediately inconsistent. But as noted in the discussion of Reductio Ad Absurdum in appendix A, it is a feature of implication that, if A is immediately inconsistent, then the proposition $P, \ldots,$ and R imply A is immediately inconsistent with the propositions $P, \ldots,$ and R. So, if one believes $P, \ldots, R$ and also believes that $P, \ldots, R$ imply A, where A is immediately inconsistent, one's beliefs are immediately inconsistent and therefore one is disposed to make changes in them to avoid this.

The Get Back Principle

I have suggested that one is motivated to resolve an indirect inconsistency in one's view only when one recognizes it, that is, only when one believes one's other beliefs are inconsistent. Given that belief, one tries to make a minimal change that eliminates the believed inconsistency, in other words, a minimal change that allows one to stop believing one's other beliefs are inconsistent. But something more needs to be said about this, otherwise the simplest modification would seem to be merely to abandon one's belief that one's other beliefs are inconsistent and to do nothing else! That would always involve a change of only one belief.

This may sometimes be the right thing to do, but not usually. One reason why not is that usually one can get back the dropped belief by reviewing the reasoning that led to it in the first place. So one could get into a pattern of accepting a belief, then rejecting it, then accepting it again, and so on. This suggests the following restriction on the rule that one should make the minimal change that eliminates one's belief that one's other beliefs are inconsistent:

> *Get Back Principle*   One should not give up a belief one can easily (and rationally) get right back.

The Get Back Principle would keep one from simply refusing to believe one's beliefs are inconsistent. It would also account for the strength of repeatable observational evidence. One tests one's views against what one perceives. If one observes something that is at variance with what one expected, then something needs to be changed. It is true that sometimes one can suppose there has been "observational error" and stick to one's original view despite the conflict with experience. But the Get Back Principle rules out simply abandoning one's observation without also concluding, for example, that there has been observational error, because the observation can then be made again giving one the same belief right back again.

Observe that the Get Back Principle cannot just say that certain combinations of beliefs are incoherent, where a given combination includes the belief that one could easily infer some proposition P or could easily come to believe that P via perception, because then one could most easily avoid the incoherence by dropping *that* belief, which is the very thing that the Get Back Principle is supposed to prevent.

The point seems to be something like this: When one revises one's views in a way that leads to certain beliefs being dropped, one is committed to the claim that there is no easy way rationally to get those beliefs right back.

There may seem to be exceptions to this, but I think they are only apparent exceptions. For example, suppose that consideration of a philosophical paradox leads one to infer something one sees to be self-contradictory (for example, "(L) is true if and only if (L) is not true"), and suppose one has no idea how to resolve the paradox. One should then certainly stop believing the self-contradictory proposition, even though it may seem that one realizes one can infer it right back from the rest of one's view. But this is not really an exception to the Get Back Principle. It is important to distinguish what is implied by one's view from what can be inferred from it. In such a situation, one sees that a self-contradictory proposition is implied by one's beliefs, but that does not mean that the proposition in question can be inferred

from one's beliefs. Since one realizes the proposition is self-contradictory, one realizes that it cannot possibly be true and so one cannot
come to believe it. It is not inferable. (Of course, "my beliefs are inconsistent" would be reinferable if one were merely to give up that
single belief.)

Furthermore, the Get Back Principle does not keep one from dropping
beliefs in whose truth one has no interest even though, given an interest
in their truth, they would be inferable. In particular, the Get Back
Principle does not keep one from forgetting one's reasons for one's
beliefs, including any observational evidence.

On the other hand, one cannot on grounds of lack of interest abandon
a belief that some of one's other beliefs are inconsistent. One always
has a reason to be interested in whether one's beliefs are inconsistent.

Measuring Minimal Changes

It seems that in changing one's view one should make minimal changes,
both in adding new beliefs and in eliminating beliefs, for example, in
order to get rid of an inconsistency in one's view. But how are such
changes to be measured?

The simplest measure would be this:

> *Simple Measure of Change in View*   Take the sum of the number
> of (explicit) new beliefs added plus the number of (explicit) old
> beliefs given up.

This measure is sensitive to the order in which inferences are made.
Suppose one starts with the following five jointly inconsistent beliefs:

> *P, Q, if P then R, if Q then R, not R.*

Using the Simple Measure, the minimal change that eliminates the
inconsistency would be to stop believing *not R*. But, if one does not
notice the inconsistency, one might first notice that *not R* and *if P then
R* imply *not P* and so infer *not P*, and similarly infer *not Q* from the
observation that *not R* and *if Q then R* imply *not Q*.

By the way, the implication from *if P then R* and *not R* to *not P* is
probably not an immediate implication, at least for most people. It
seems to take most people longer to recognize it than to recognize true
immediate implications. One might have to notice that adding the
additional assumption *P* to *if P then R* and *not R* leads to inconsistency,
and then infer *not P* by Reductio Ad Absurdum.

Anyway, if one did thus infer *not P* and *not Q*, one would have the
following beliefs:

> *P, Q, if P then R, if Q then R, not R, not P, not Q.*

At this point, the minimal change which eliminates the inconsistency consists in giving up two beliefs, P and Q. There is no longer any way to get rid of the inconsistency by abandoning belief in *not R* without also giving up at least two other beliefs, for example, *not P* and *not Q*. So giving up *not R* would not be part of a minimal change at this later stage.

This effect of the order in which inferences are made may seem implausible, but it is characteristic of a coherence approach (in contrast to the foundations theory) that the order of inference can matter in this sort of way, since in a coherence approach no record has to be kept of one's reasons for one's beliefs.

In a foundations approach we could modify the Simple Measure and say that, if giving up one belief would eliminate one's justification for believing a second, then, since giving up the first belief would require giving up the second as well, the giving up of these two beliefs should be counted as (what is involved in) the loss of only one belief, not two separate beliefs. In this approach one should count only those beliefs given up that are not forced to be given up by the giving up of their justifications. Using this modified measure, the minimal change in the last example would be to give up *not R*. Although this would require also giving up *not P* and *not Q*, this would count as a one-belief change, rather than a three-belief change.

This way of putting things presupposes the unacceptable Principle of Negative Undermining. One is supposed to associate justifications with one's beliefs and abandon beliefs that lose their justifications. The corresponding suggestion, given the more acceptable Principle of Positive Undermining, would be that, if one believes P, Q, and P is one's *only reason to believe* Q, then giving up P and Q should count as a change of one belief rather than a change of two.

It is not clear whether the Simple Measure should be modified in accordance with this suggestion. If the Simple Measure is accepted, "central" beliefs, defined as beliefs one takes to be a crucial part of one's reason for many other beliefs, will be much more protected from being given up than they would be if the principle were modified. The Principle of Positive Undermining would allow such a central belief B to be given up only if either one stops believing that one's justifications for these other beliefs depend on one's belief in B or one stops believing the various beliefs one thinks depend on B for their justification. In either case, extensive changes must be made to one's view. According to the Simple Measure of Change in View, we are to count each of these changes as an additional mark against changing B, which can make it harder to give up B than to give up some less central belief. According to the suggested revision, however, we are to count the whole change as a change of one, which makes it much easier to give up B. So, the original measure would protect central beliefs in a way that the revision would not. It is unclear whether central beliefs should be protected in this way. It might be suggested that principles of logic and mathematics owe their relative unrevisability to being central in this respect. But this is a matter that needs detailed examination, and I have no idea what the outcome of such an examination will be.

In the discussion that follows, I appeal to the Simple Measure of counting *all* the (explicit) beliefs given up or added; but this does not matter in the one case I discuss in which the measure is applied, since the same results would emerge if the measure were modified.

Long-Term versus Momentary Acceptance

It is possibly relevant whether inference would lead one to accept a proposition as something to be remembered or only for the moment, in the course of a longer argument. If one's interest in knowing whether Q is true derives from an interest in knowing whether something else, P, is true, one has an interest in noting *for the moment* whether Q is true. After one comes to accept P, one does not have to keep accepting Q, since the foundations theory is false.

Momentary acceptance is certainly less of a worry than long-term acceptance from the point of view of clutter avoidance. This conflicts with the Simple Measure of Change in View, since momentary acceptance would get counted as two changes—adding something now and deleting it in a moment. Part of the solution here is not to count forgetting (that is, giving up something in which one is no longer interested) as inference that is subject to the principle of minimizing change in view. We might also want to count momentary additions as of less weight than long-term additions.

There is still a practical reason to minimize even short-term changes. Short arguments are easier to handle and use fewer resources than longer arguments. In what follows I will not modify the Simple Measure to give more weight to long-term changes, although again this will not affect the one case I discuss.

Simplicity

The Simple Measure of Change in View considers only the number of changed beliefs. It does not take the complexity of those beliefs directly into account. However, it appears that the measure favors simple hypotheses over more complicated hypotheses.

Suppose one is interested in determining a certain function F, given the following evidence:

$$F(17) = 34,$$
$$F(23) = 46,$$
$$F(36) = 72,$$
$$F(41) = 82.$$

Consider two hypotheses:

(H1) $F(n) = 2n$,
(H2) $F(n) = 2n + (n - 17)(n - 23)(n - 36)(n - 41)$.

Both hypotheses would explain the data, but we would normally suppose the first is more reasonable because it is simpler. I suggest that the difference is reflected in the amount of short-term change in view the hypotheses require. (H2) is less conservative than (H1).

To show this, I must anticipate what I say in chapter 7 and suppose that one would come to accept a hypothesis of this sort only as part of an explanation of the data. Then, to use (H1) to explain the data, one needs to infer

$F(17)$	$= 2 \times 17$	(implied by (H1)),
$2 \times 17 = 34$		(obvious arithmetical consequence),
$F(23)$	$= 2 \times 23$	(implied by (H1)),
$2 \times 23 = 46$		(obvious arithmetical consequence),
etc.		

This explanation involves adding eight momentary beliefs in addition to (H1).

To use (H2) to explain the data, one similarly needs to infer such intermediate propositions as the following:

$$F(17) = 2 \times 17 + (17 - 17)(17 - 23)(17 - 36)(17 - 41),$$
$$2 \times 17 + (17 - 17)(17 - 23)(17 - 36)(17 - 41) = 34.$$

The second equation is an arithmetical truth, but let us suppose it is not an *immediate* consequence of arithmetical principles one accepts. In order to get to it, one needs to do some slight reasoning, involving the acceptance of the following principles:

$$17 - 17 = 0.$$

So

$$(17 - 17)(17 - 23)(17 - 36)(17 - 41) = 0.$$

So

$$2 \times 17 + (17 - 17)(17 - 23)(17 - 36)(17 - 41) = 2 \times 17.$$
$$2 \times 17 = 34.$$

So

$$2 \times 17 + (17 - 17)(17 - 23)(17 - 36)(17 - 41) = 34.$$

This last proposition is the needed consequence.

In order to explain the data using (H2), we must, at least for the short term, accept five intermediate steps for each of the the four items of data in addition to (H2) itself. This involves accepting $4 \times 5 = 20$ momentary beliefs. The short-term change is therefore over twice as much as for (H1) (20 beliefs *versus* 8 beliefs), whereas the added coherence is, let us suppose, about the same. So the simpler hypothesis (H1) involves less change in view, given the Simple Measure of Change in View, which merely totals the number of added and subtracted beliefs.

Summary

The Interest Condition on theoretical reasoning says one has a reason to add a new belief only if one is (or has a reason to be) interested in whether the belief is true. One can have a reason to be interested in whether a belief is true if that might facilitate practical or theoretical reasoning in which one is (or has a reason to be) interested. One can be (or have a reason to be) interested in whether Q is true without being (or having a reason to be) interested in whether *not* Q is true. One always has a reason to be interested in whether one's beliefs are inconsistent.

The Get Back Principle says that one should not give up something one can easily infer right back. Given one's interest in whether one's beliefs are inconsistent, this makes it difficult to forget about inconsistencies one has discovered. It also accounts for the strength of repeatable observational evidence. (But, since one does not have to be interested in the observational evidence, it is usually OK to forget about it once one has gone on to draw from it conclusions in which one is interested.)

There are practical reasons to minimize change in one's view. In changing one's views, one should make minimal changes. It is not clear what the appropriate measure of the size of change is. Simply counting the explicit beliefs added and given up is a possible measure, although it may be wise to modify this so as not to count beliefs given up because of Positive Undermining, and we should probably treat adding new long-term beliefs as more of a change than adding new temporary beliefs.

There is probably no need to take the complexity of particular beliefs into account, since acceptance of more complicated beliefs also seems to involve the acceptance of more beliefs, period.

Chapter 7
Explanatory Coherence

I have suggested that the coherence of one's view can be a factor in reasoning. In reasoning one attempts in part to make one's view more coherent, subject to other constraints, such as conservatism and the Get Back Principle. In this chapter I want to say something about the relevant sort of coherence.

Coherence in a view consists in connections of intelligibility among the elements of the view. Among other things these include explanatory connections, which hold when part of one's view makes it intelligible to one why some other part should be true. In such a case one believes not only P, Q, and R but also R *because P and Q*.

Some connections of intelligibility are immediate. One immediately grasps how certain things do or might explain others. For example, a relation of immediate intelligibility might hold for one between the belief that *all crows are black* and the belief that *this crow is black*. Similarly, such a relation might hold between, on the one hand, the two beliefs *this is an emerald* and *all emeralds are green* and, on the other hand, the belief *this is green*. Again, going back to an example discussed in chapter 6, a relation of immediate intelligibility might connect one's beliefs that, *for all n, $F(n) = 2n$; $2 \times 17 = 34$;* and *$F(17) = 34$*. Finally, to take an example in which such a connection is not deductive, a relation of immediate intelligibility might connect one's beliefs that *the sugar was stirred into the tea* and that *sugar is soluble in tea* with one's belief that *the sugar dissolved in the tea*. (The connection in this last case is not deductive since the latter belief could be false even though the former beliefs were true.)

Explanatory "Arguments"

Explanations may involve several steps or "subexplanations," so the representation linking various beliefs together might look like this:

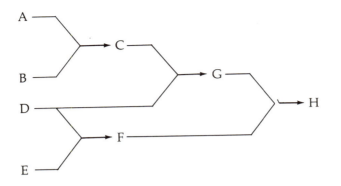

This sort of pattern of links among beliefs resembles the sort of pattern required in a foundations theory of justification. The arrows here represent links of *explanation* rather than links of *justification*, and there is no constant relation between these notions. As we shall see, one's acceptance of an explanatory link between *P* and *Q* might originally have been the result of an inference from either a previous belief in *P* or a previous belief in *Q* (or both).

As this sort of diagram indicates, some explanatory connections are immediate, whereas others are indirect, involving something like argument. We can therefore distinguish three cases in which one believes *P because Q*:

1. One finds the connection between *P* and *Q* to be "immediately intelligible."
2. One accepts an explanatory argument linking *P* and *Q* with a series of immediately intelligible connections.
3. Neither case 1 nor case 2 applies: One explicitly believes *P because Q* but has forgotten or never was aware of immediately intelligible links connecting *P* with *Q*. However, in this case there is an immediately intelligible connection between one's beliefs that *Q* and that *P because Q* on the one hand and one's belief that *P* on the other hand.

If we think of the arrows as representing immediately intelligible connections, then case 3 might involve this:

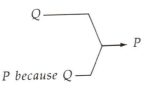

In this case one explicitly believes *P because Q*. In cases 1 and 2 one might believe this only implicitly by virtue of the links of immediate intelligibility that hold among one's beliefs.

Two Concepts of Explanation

The term "explanation" is used to refer to different sorts of things. Sometimes by an explanation one means the speech act of explaining something to someone; at other times one means instead something one grasps or understands that makes things more intelligible, comprehensible, or coherent, whether or not any speech act of explaining has occurred.

In what follows, I use the term "explanation" always in the second sense, to refer to something one understands that makes one's view more coherent and intelligible. I do not mean the speech act of explaining.

Furthermore, the relevant explanations are always of the form *R because P, . . . , and Q*, explaining *why* or how it is that something is so. Achinstein (1983) points out that there are other sorts of explanations. Examples include explaining what a word means, explaining what someone's intentions are, and perhaps explaining who someone is. These other sorts of explanations do not seem by themselves to involve the relevant sorts of coherence increasing connections of intelligibility, except where they also include explaining why something is so. Therefore, in what follows, I use the term "explanation" always to refer to explanations of why or how it is that something is the case.

Inference to an Explanation

"Inference to the best explanation" occurs when one infers something that might explain the evidence. One starts by believing *e* and comes to believe *e because h*. For example, a mother hears a shuffling noise from upstairs and concludes she has forgotten to close the gate on the stairs so that her one-year-old child has been able to climb up to the second floor and make the shuffling noise that she hears. A detective infers the best explanation of the evidence, namely, that the butler did it. A scientist concludes from a photograph that a certain sort of particle interaction has occurred. From what a speaker says, one infers that the speaker believes *P*, in other words, one infers that the speaker's having this belief is part of the reason why the speaker said what he or she said. From Mary's actions, one infers that she intends to be in New York tomorrow, that is, one infers that her having this intention explains her actions.

I say this is inference to the "best" explanation because the explanation one infers should be the best of competing explanations. At least, it should be the best of competing explanations at the same "level." There might be a competing explanation that is better but that involves an improved version of some theory which one could not have been expected to think of. That would not keep one from being justified in reaching the conclusion one reached.

Satisficing and Maximizing

Belief revision is like a game in which one tries to make minimal changes that improve one's position. One loses points for every change and gains points for every increase in coherence. One does not normally try to maximize. One tries to get a "satisfactory" improvement in one's score. One "satisfices" rather than maximizes (Simon 1969).

I have already mentioned an exception to the general policy of satisficing. One does try to accept the best of competing hypotheses at the same level. We must distinguish choosing among competitors at the same level, where one is restricted to taking the best, from choosing between smaller and larger changes in one's view which do not necessarily involve competing hypotheses. In the latter case it is OK to satisfice.

Theoretical and practical reasoning differ in this respect. In practical reasoning one can be justified in satisficing even in choosing among competing plans at the same level. In fact, often this is just what one should do—make an arbitrary choice of a satisfactory plan to accomplish one's goals. But in theoretical reasoning one would not be justified in making an arbitrary choice of what to believe among competing hypotheses at the same level.

Inference from an Explanation

In other cases one infers an explanation of the conclusion. One starts by believing *e* and comes to believe *h because e*. From the trajectory of the bomb and the position of the target one infers the bomb will miss; that is, one infers that the current position and momentum of the bomb will lead it to miss the target. From Mary's intention to be in New York tomorrow, one infers that she will be in New York tomorrow; that is, one infers that her intention will result in her being in New York. Similarly, because of its solubility, the sugar will dissolve in the tea.

Nondeductive Explanation

I have already remarked that explanations do not have to be "deductive." One might conclude, from the facts that one is stirring sugar into one's hot tea and that sugar is soluble in tea, that the sugar will dissolve in the tea. Or one might conclude from the fact that there is dissolved sugar in the tea that this is because someone has stirred in sugar. There is a single explanation here, inferred in different ways. But one cannot express this explanation as a deductive argument. The explanation is defeasible. It holds only "other things being equal." The sugar would not dissolve (or would not have dissolved) if it were (or had been) coated with wax or if there were (or had been) already a saturated solution in the tea or if other conditions had obtained, some of which one could not now even envision (such as strange magnetic fields, perhaps).

Similarly, when one infers that Mary's intention will (or did) lead to her being in New York, one's explanation holds only "other things being equal," since Mary's intention would not lead (or have led) to her being in New York if she came (or had come) to change her mind or if she were (or had been) prevented by circumstances from getting to New York.

It might be suggested that these explanations can be turned into deductive arguments by adding the premise that "other things are equal." The relevant arguments might look like this:

> The sugar is stirred into the tea.
> If other things are equal, sugar dissolves when stirred in tea.
> Other things are equal.
> So the sugar dissolves.

> Mary intends to be in New York tomorrow.
> Other things being equal, people do what they intend.
> Other things are equal.
> So Mary will be in New York tomorrow.

However, this does not work, since "other things being equal" does not simply report a single possible situation that might obtain. Other things might be equal with respect to the sugar's dissolving in the tea without other things' being equal with respect to Mary's doing what she intends and being in New York tomorrow. We cannot just suppose that, since the first explanation is correct, it is true that other things are equal, so the second explanation is also correct.

Hempel, who has been one of the most important defenders of the deductive nomological model of scientific explanation (Hempel 1965), has recently suggested (in unpublished work) that all serious scientific explanations are nondeductive in this way. They all contain implicit or explicit "provisos" concerning the absence of interruptions, including those of a sort that cannot be specified in the terminology of the theory used in the explanation.

Statistical Inference and Statistical Explanation

Given the frequency with which six comes up when one throws a particular die, one infers the die is "loaded" so as to favor side six. This is to reason from the observed evidence to a statistical explanation of that evidence. One concludes that the best explanation of the observed evidence is that the probability of getting a six on tossing this die is greater than one out of six. One infers that the observed frequency of sixes has occurred because the die is loaded.

Such a statistical explanation is nondeductive. From a description of the antecedent situation there is no way to deduce how the die will actually come up in a series of tosses, even though one can *infer* such a description in the other direction, from the observation of the resulting series of tosses.

We can appeal to this connection between explanation and reasoning in order to resolve certain issues in the theory of statistical explanation. For example, consider the dispute as to whether a statistical explanation of an outcome must show that the outcome was "to be expected" by giving it a high statistical probability given the initial conditions. Hempel (1965) says yes. Jeffrey (1969) says no. My approach leads me to side with Jeffrey. Statistical explanations do not have to show that the resulting event was statistically probable. When one infers from an observed sequence of tosses that a die is biased toward six, one does not suppose that, with such a bias, that particular observed sequence of tosses was highly probable. In fact, that particular sequence of tosses was highly improbable even with the biased die! However, the explanation citing a biased die is "better" than an explanation appealing to an unbiased die in the sense of "more inferable," because the sequence of tosses actually obtained would have been much more improbable on the latter hypothesis than on the former.

The Lottery Paradox Again

Can one infer something simply because it is statistically highly probable, given the evidence? That would be an inference from an explanation, an inference to a conclusion of the form *h because e*, which we have seen is a possible sort of inference. But to suppose one can make such an inference on statistical grounds would seem to yield the lottery paradox. Although one believes that one ticket will win, one could also infer, for any ticket in the lottery that *that ticket* won't be the winning ticket.

There is no actual contradiction here. To say one can infer this of any ticket is not to say one can infer it of all. Given that one has inferred ticket number 1 will not win, then one must suppose the odds against ticket number 2 are no longer 999,999 to 1, but only 999,998 to 1. And after one infers ticket number 2 won't win, one must change the odds on ticket number 3 to 999,997 to 1, and so on. If one could get to ticket number 999,999, one would have to suppose the odds were even, 1 to 1, so at that point the hypothesis that this ticket will not win would be no better than the hypothesis that it will win, and one could infer no further. (Presumably one would have to have stopped before this point.) But the order of inference *really* matters here, since one could have inferred that ticket 999,999 won't win if only one had made this last inference early enough. And, although we have seen that it is characteristic of a coherence approach that the order of inference matters, that is because one may forget one's reasons for believing something. Here, the order of inference matters even if one fully re-members one's reasons.

Knowledge

Could such a statistical inference give one knowledge if it is in this direction, from an explanation to a conclusion? If it is a fair lottery, can one *know* this particular ticket will not be the winning ticket? This can seem wrong.

Yet an inference in the other direction, from observed evidence to a statistical explanation of the evidence, can give one knowledge. If one tosses the die again and again, one can come to know that the probability of six on this die is closer to 1/2 than to 1/6. What is the difference? Why is knowledge clearly possible in the one case and not clearly possible in the other?

Suppose Bill wants to know where Mary will be tomorrow. Bill knows that Mary intends to be in New York. Bill also knows that if Mary's ticket is the winning ticket, she will instead be in Trenton for the award ceremony. But there is only one chance in a million of that. Can't Bill conclude that Mary will be in New York tomorrow and in that way come to know where Mary will be tomorrow? That seems possible. But doesn't it involve knowing her lottery ticket is not going to be a winning ticket?

Perhaps, it makes a difference what question is being considered: "Which ticket will win?" versus "Where will Mary be tomorrow?" Perhaps this affects which alternatives are being considered; and one tries for the best alternative (Levi 1967). This may be so, but it does not account for our reluctance to say one knows the ticket is not the winning ticket, since we are reluctant when we are not interested in which ticket will win but only in whether *this* ticket will win.

I have no idea how to account for our reluctance to attribute knowledge in cases of this sort.

Nonstatistical Nondeterministic Explanation

There seem to be nondeterministic explanations that are not statistical. Psychological explanation may be of this sort. One explains what led a person to act as he or she did, how it happened that there was such a result, without any appeal to either deterministic or even statistical laws connecting the initial situation to the action.

Such explanations can support inference to the best explanation. One can infer that a person is acting in a certain way because he or she has certain beliefs and desires, without supposing that there are deterministic or statistical laws leading from those beliefs and desires to those actions.

Implication and Explanation

Implication and explanation are both coherence giving. Both immediate implications and immediate explanations are "immediately intelligible." Is there then a single underlying principle?

If all explanations were deductive, the coherence-giving quality of explanation might be derived from the coherence-giving quality of implication. But, as we have seen, there are nondeductive explanations, including statistical explanations, explanations that appeal to "other things being equal" (as in the explanation of the sugar's dissolving in the tea), and nondeterministic nonstatistical explanations, such as grammatical and psychological explanations.

Does it go the other way? Does the coherence-giving quality of implication derive from that of explanation? Are all implications explanatory? At first, it may seem not. For one thing, any proposition implies itself, but this is not to say that any proposition is self-explanatory.

True, this implication is not coherence giving in the relevant sense either. One cannot come to be justified in believing a proposition simply by deducing it from itself. But there are other cases in which nonexplanatory implications do seem to be coherence giving. One can come to be justified in reaching a conclusion by means of a deductive argument that does not seem to be explanatory. For example, one might reach a conclusion about the angle of the sun relative to the horizon by deducing it from information about the height of a particular flagpole, the length of its shadow, and certain optical and geometrical principles, where this does not seem to involve any sort of explanation of the sun's being at that angle. (Bromberger 1966)

Similarly, suppose one believes Trudy leaves her car in her garage whenever she is home. On looking in the garage and discovering the car is not there, one infers that Trudy is not home. The relevant implication here goes from "If Trudy is home, Trudy's car is in the garage" and "Trudy's car is not in the garage" to "Trudy is not home." This implication is sufficiently coherence giving to allow one to make the inference, but it does not seem to explain why Trudy is not home.

On the other hand appearances may be deceiving. There are explanations and explanations. Sometimes one explains S by citing some prior events that caused or brought about or led up to S. But other explanations are not like this. Newton's explanation of Kepler's laws is not of that form. Rather, it shows how the approximate truth of Kepler's laws follows from more general principles. Perhaps the implication concerning Trudy's whereabouts is explanatory but not a causal explanation.

Steven's daughter Tess asks him why Olivia is her cousin. Steven explains that Olivia is the daughter of his sister and that one's cousins include any children of one's parent's brothers or sisters. This explanation too does not seem to be a causal explanation. Perhaps one has an explanation of Trudy's absence that is like this.

Again, some mathematical proofs seem more explanatory than others, where the relevant sort of explanation is not causal. Steiner (1978) contrasts two different ways to show that

$$1 + 2 + \ldots + n = n(n + 1)/2.$$

PROOF 1. The theorem can be proved by mathematical induction if (a) the theorem can be shown to hold for $n = 1$ and (b) it can be shown that, if the theorem holds for any given number n, it also holds for the next number $n + 1$. This can be done as follows: If $n = 1$, the theorem holds, since $1 = (1 \times 2)/2$. Furthermore, if we assume the theorem holds for any given n, we can show it holds for $n + 1$, for then

$$
\begin{aligned}
1 + 2 + \ldots + n + (n + 1) &= n(n + 1)/2 + (n + 1) \\
&= n(n + 1)/2 + 2(n + 1)/2 \\
&= (n + 1)(n + 2)/2.
\end{aligned}
$$

QED.

PROOF 2: We can add the series of numbers from 1 to n to itself reversed, in the following way:

$$
\begin{array}{ccccccccc}
1 & + & 2 & + \ldots + & (n-1) & + & n \\
n & + & (n-1) & + \ldots + & 2 & + & 1 \\
\hline
(n+1) & + & (n+1) & + \ldots + & (n+1) & + & (n+1)
\end{array}
$$

There are n terms in the bottom series, so the sum of that series is clearly $n(n+1)$. Since that is the sum of the original series taken twice, we have to divide by 2 to get the sum of the original series taken once, $n(n+1)/2$. QED.

The second proof seems more explanatory than the first proof. It makes it intelligible why the theorem holds in a way that the first proof does not. It would be interesting to try to say why the second proof is more explanatory than the first. I have not tried to do that. Part of the reason for the more explanatory nature of proof 2 may be that it "motivates" the theorem by allowing us to use the proof to discover what the theorem is, whereas proof 1, using mathematical induction, is possible only if we already know what the theorem is. But why is that relevant to how explanatory the proof is? My present point is merely that it seems to make sense to consider one proof as more explanatory than another, where the relevant sort of explanation is not causal explanation.

Noncausal explanations are sometimes relatively weak or trivial, and there are sometimes disputes as to whether a given case is a case of explanation. Is there any explanatory force to the claim that a particular person's taking opium on a particular occasion put that person to sleep because opium has a dormative virtue? Yes, the claim has some force. One sees the particular case as an instance of a more general phenomenon, taking opium tends to put a person to sleep. This is not as trivial as saying that taking opium puts people to sleep because opium has a dormative virtue. That would be like explaining P by citing P itself.

Is there explanatory force to the claim that the sun came up this morning because it always does or to the claim that this bird is black because it is a crow and all crows are black? These are disputed points. I suggest that we can take these to be noncausal explanations of a relatively weak sort.

Consider the previous argument whose conclusion is that Trudy is not home. That argument does not seem to be explanatory. But perhaps this is because it is a weak noncausal explanation. Similarly for Bromberger's flagpole case. Perhaps the argument provides a kind of noncausal explanation of the angle of the sun, even though it does not offer a causal explanation of why the sun should be at that angle.

Perhaps this is the sort of explanation that figures, for example, in explaining why Tess and Olivia are cousins.

This does not absolutely establish that the relevance to reasoning of implication is a special case of the relevance of explanatory coherence, but it indicates that this may be so or at least that it may be possible to say this without stretching language too far.

Summary

The coherence in a view depends on relations of immediate coherence or intelligibility among elements in the view. Explanatory coherence is an important sort of coherence, perhaps the only sort. It allows one to infer something that best explains the evidence and also something that will be best explained by things one already believes. One does not have to maximize by finding absolutely the best modification in one's view, but if one infers an explanation, that must be the best of competing explanations at the "same level." (Here theoretical and practical reasoning diverge.) Explanations can be deductive or nondeductive. They can be statistical. One can infer a certain outcome of a chance setup if the statistical probability of that outcome is great enough, although there are complications in the case of lotteries, perhaps because one *hopes* to win despite the odds. Nondeductive explanations can be statistical or nondeterministic and nonstatistical as in linguistics or in commonsense psychology. Finally, although there appear to be cases in which there are relations of coherence that support inference that are not explanatory, this appearance may rest on a failure to remember that there are explanations that are not causal, as in mathematical explanations or Newton's explanation of Kepler's laws.

Chapter 8

Revising Intentions: Some Preliminary
Considerations

I understand practical reasoning to be the reasoned revision of intentions. I stress this because the phrase "practical reasoning" is often used in other ways. For example, as I observed in chapter 1, it is sometimes used to refer to a peculiar sort of argument, a practical syllogism or an argument in the logic of imperatives. But principles of reasoned revision are not the same sort of thing as principles of syllogism or logic.

The phrase "practical reasoning" is also sometimes used to refer to reasoning about what one *ought* to do or about what one has *reasons* to do (Nagel 1970; Williams 1980). That is really a particular kind of theoretical reasoning, given the way in which I am distinguishing theoretical from practical reasoning, since reasoning that is concerned with what to believe about what one ought to do or with what one has reasons to do is still reasoning concerned with what one ought to believe. (I say more about *ought, reasons,* and judgments about practical reasoning in appendix B.)

Some of the basic principles of practical reasoning, treated as the reasoned revision of intentions, are similar to the basic principles of theoretical reasoning, treated as the reasoned revision of beliefs. On the one hand there is a principle of *conservatism,* which says to minimize changes in one's intentions; on the other hand there is a principle of *coherence,* which encourages changes that would make one's intentions more coherent wth each other and with one's beliefs and which discourages changes that would make them less coherent.

For practical reasoning there is also a distinctive principle of *desire satisfaction,* which encourages changes that promise to promote the realization of one's ends and which discourages changes that promise frustration of these ends. Although one's desires can be relevant to theoretical reasoning by affecting whether one has a reason to be interested in a given issue, the desire that a particular conclusion C should be true is not an acceptable theoretical reason to believe that C rather than the contrary is true in the way that such a desire can be a practical reason to form the intention of making C true.

Nagel (1970) denies that one's desires themselves play a special role in practical reasoning. He argues that it is one's beliefs about one's desires that are relevant. He goes on to argue that one's future desires and the desires of others are as relevant to one's practical reasoning as one's own present desires are, although desires are always relevant only through one's beliefs about them. Nagel's view about this may be in part the result of his conflating practical reasoning in my sense, that is, reasoning that revises plans and intentions, with theoretical reasoning about how one ought to revise one's plans and intentions. One's current desires should not influence the outcome of this latter sort of theoretical reasoning in the way that they can and must influence the actual revising of one's plans and intentions.

I try to be more specific about the principles of practical reasoning in what follows. At the same time, since practical reasoning is in the first instance concerned with intentions rather than beliefs, I also need to say something about what intentions are.

Explicit Intentions

First, and most important, I want to suggest that intentions are like beliefs in being either explicit or implicit. That is, I claim that explicit intention is a distinctive kind of psychological attitude, different from desire, belief, hope, fear, and so forth. In particular, I deny that one's intentions are merely implicit in one's beliefs or desires.

In my view intentions can be characterized at least partly by saying how they function in reasoning and action. Intentions can lead in a characteristic way to actions. Furthermore, they arise from and are modified by practical reasoning. In particular, one's current intentions play an important role in practical reasoning; this role differs from the role played by desires or beliefs. It is important that intentions typically are not momentary states but endure from the time of decision to the time of intended action, although they can, of course, be modified by later reasoning and abandoned if one changes one's mind or forgets.

Against this, some writers argue that intentions *are* merely implicit in beliefs and desires. But I believe this contrary view cannot be supported. For example, Beardsley (1978) holds that one intends to do something if and only if one consciously believes one will do it and also consciously wants to do it. I do not object to the assumption here that one intends to do something only if one believes one will do it, although many disagree with that assumption. I discuss that issue subsequently. Quite apart from that issue, Beardsley's thesis yields counterintuitive results concerning cases in which one wants to do something and believes one will do it but does not believe that doing it will result from wanting to do it. For example, suppose Jeff is about to blow pepper into Sam's face. If Sam believes he will sneeze as a result of this and if he wants to sneeze, Beardsley's account implies that Sam intends to sneeze and his resulting sneeze is intentional! This strikes me and almost everyone else as clearly wrong.

Davidson (1963) avoids this last result, that the sneeze is intentional, by requiring that an intentional action be *caused* by the relevant desire and belief. In this view if one does something because one has a dominant desire for G and believes one's action will result in G, that constitutes intending to G. But, as Davidson (1978) observes, this simpleminded causal analysis does not work either. There are two problems. The first is that the causal connection between one's belief and desire and one's action must be restricted in some way to avoid counterexamples. To adapt an example of Davidson (1973), a mountain climber might want her partner to fall, and might believe that letting go of the rope would cause her partner to fall, without intending to cause her partner to fall, even if the belief and desire make her so excited that she unintentionally lets go of the rope. This suggests that a belief and a desire determine an intention only if they lead one to act in the relevant way by leading one to *intend*: to get G by acting in the relevant way.

The second problem with the simpleminded causal analysis in Davidson (1963) is that it says nothing about intentions to do something at a later time, intentions which have not yet led to action and may never lead to action. Since it has nothing to say about the distinctive way such current intentions affect later intentions, the account cannot adequately characterize what intentions are.

Davidson (1978) attempts to deal with this by identifying an intention with an all-out evaluation, judging that a certain course of action is best. This would appear to identify intention with a certain sort of belief, namely, the belief that a certain course of action is best; however, Davidson also says that the relevant sort of evaluation is or expresses a "pro-attitude," where desires are also pro-attitudes. So he takes an intention to be a kind of belief that is similar to a desire. (In my view evaluations of this sort are not themselves pro-attitudes, although they may be beliefs about what pro-attitudes there are reasons to take. See appendix B.) Clearly, this is to allow for explicit intentions that are not implicit in ordinary beliefs and desires and to agree that in this respect intentions are a particular kind of mental state in their own right.

Positive, Negative, and Conditional Intentions

An intention to do *A* is a *positive intention* if it involves the thought that it will lead one to do *A*. If one intends to go to a certain place at a certain time, one normally supposes one would not be going to that place at that time except for having formed the intention to go. One envisions oneself going to that place at that time because of, and only because of, one's intention.

In thinking about intention, it is tempting to think all intentions are positive intentions. But there are other kinds of intention as well. In particular, there are cases in which one forms an intention to do something, *A*, without supposing one would not do *A* in the absence of this intention and without supposing one's intention will lead one to do *A*. For example, one decides *not* to go to a certain place at a certain time—one decides not to go to the party tonight. Normally, in such a case, one does not think one would end up at the party in the absence of a firm intention not to go. One would have that thought only if one had actively to prevent oneself from being taken to the party or one had to take firm steps to counteract a strong temptation to go. But that is not the usual case. Normally, one supposes one would go to the party only if one had a definite positive intention to go. Normally, one thinks one would not go if one had formed no intention either way.

Why then does one bother to form the intention not to go? Perhaps because one needs to decide that question in order to settle certain other issues such as where to have dinner, whether to obtain a copy of tonight's TV schedule, and so forth. In this case, then, one forms the intention of not going to the party without supposing one's intention will lead one not to go. (One supposes only that one's intention settles that issue.)

Let us call an intention like this a *negative intention*, with the understanding that this does not mean the content of the intention is explicitly negative. The intention *to stay home tonight* will be a negative intention as long as one does not think of the intention as being responsible for one's staying home tonight, even though the content of the intention is not explicitly negative. On the other hand, even though the content of the intention *not* to remain at the party for more than an hour is explicitly negative, the intention itself is probably a positive one, since one probably forms the intention in order to get oneself not to stay beyond an hour at the party.

One way to test whether an intention, such as the intention to stay home, is a negative intention is to consider whether in intending to stay home one aims at staying home and also to consider whether one has a plan in order to ensure that one stays home. Normally, one does not aim at staying home, nor does one have a plan for staying home. That indicates one's intention is a negative one: one does not see one's intention as instrumental in getting one to do as one intends. On the other hand, if one forms the intention to stay home in order to resist the temptation to go, then one does aim at staying home and may have to plan what to do in order not to give in. In that case, one's intention is a positive intention: one sees it as instrumental in leading one to do as one intends.

Conditional intentions are an intermediate case. One intends to go to the party if Bobby calls to say he is going. One does not envision one's intention leading one to do something unless Bobby calls—only in that case does one envision it as affecting how one acts. Kent Bach has pointed out to me that this is an example of what might be called a conditional positive intention and that there are also conditional negative intentions: one intends to go to the party unless Bobby calls to say he is going. There may be further complications here; I do not know. In any event I consider only ordinary positive and negative intentions in what follows.

In order to see how it complicates matters to allow for negative and conditional intentions as well as positive intentions, consider Davidson's (1978) identification of intentions with "all out" evaluative judgments. How is this to avoid counting as intentions mere hopes that something will happen, for example, when one hopes another person will blow pepper in one's face? One might very well make some sort of all-out evaluative judgment in favor of that event without being in a position to intend it to occur. So, it would seem that only some all-out evaluative judgments can count as intentions. Which ones? Here it is tempting to identify intentions with evaluative judgments made about events one conceives as one's intentional actions, that is, about those events one conceives of as the upshot of one's intention, or, to get rid of circularity here, those events one conceives of as the upshot of one's making the all-out evaluative judgment in question. But at best, this would work only for positive intentions. It would not allow for negative and conditional intentions, since on forming those intentions one does not conceive of the favored event as the upshot of one's intending as one does.

The account in Grice (1972) is subject to a similar objection. Grice appeals to a notion of *willing that one should do A,* a notion which is in certain respects similar to what Davidson (1978) calls an all-out evaluative judgment in favor of *A*-ing. Grice then identifies *intending* to do *A* with simultaneously willing that one should do *A* while believing one will do *A* as a result of so willing.

This involves the controversial assumption already mentioned in connection with Beardsley (1978), namely, that intending to do *A* implies believing one will do *A*. I do not object to that, since I believe the assumption should be accepted (but see the following discussion). My objection is that Grice's analysis of intending works at best only for positive intentions. In the case of a negative intention one does not believe one's act will be the result of willing to do as one intends.

Maybe Grice could weaken his claim and say that, in the case of a negative intention to do *A*, one believes that one's willing settles it that one is going to do *A*. And, recalling the discussion of explanation in chapter 7, we might say one believes one will do *A* because one intends to do *A*. One can believe one's intention explains one's doing *A* even if one does not believe it gives a causal explanation of one's doing *A*.

Coherence

Just as it is inconsistent to believe one will do both *A* and *B* if one also believes one cannot do both, it is also inconsistent to intend to do both *A* and *B* if one believes one cannot do both. And, just as one might be unjustified in believing something will occur without also having some idea why it will occur, one might also be unjustified in intending to do something if one has no idea of how one will do it.

As a result of an inference from an explanation, one might be justified in coming to believe one will receive a check for a thousand dollars in the mail tomorrow. For example, one might reason that one is owed a royalty payment of a thousand dollars, that payments are mailed on the first of the month, and that it takes two days for mail to get from the publisher to one's house, tomorrow being the third. Or one might be expecting one's salary check. But one would not normally be justified in coming to believe one was going to receive a check for a thousand dollars in the mail tomorrow unless one had some idea of why this would happen.

There are apparent exceptions to this. Perhaps a trustworthy person has told one to expect such a check in tomorrow's mail without saying why. Or perhaps one has noticed a pattern in which each day someone else on the block has received such a check, and one is next in line. In such cases one's new belief must still cohere with one's other beliefs, even if it is not explained by them in any profound way. (An explanation might be relevant even in these cases. Perhaps in the first case one believes one's friend is aware of something that will explain the appearance of the check, and perhaps in the second case one accepts the low-level explanation that one will receive the check because of the pattern.)

One would definitely *not* be justified in coming to believe one will receive a check for a thousand dollars in tomorrow's mail if this failed to cohere in any way with one's other beliefs, so that not only had one no idea of why one would receive such a check, but also one has not been told to expect such a check by a reliable friend, one has not noticed a relevant pattern of such things, and so on.

Similarly, while in New Jersey, Pam might be justified in forming an intention to be in California tomorrow if she has some sort of plan for getting there. Perhaps she has her own private airplane and plans to fly to Los Angeles tonight. Or Pam plans to take a scheduled airline flight from Newark to San Francisco. But Pam would not normally be justified in forming such an intention if she had no idea how she was going to get to California.

Again there are apparent exceptions. A reliable friend might promise that he will see to it that Pam gets there, although he does not say how he will do it. Or Pam might simply be able to rely on her own ability to figure out a way to get there as time goes on. In such cases Pam's intentions still sufficiently cohere with each other and with her other beliefs to allow her to form the intention. And Pam does have a plan of sorts. Her plan is to rely on her friend or on her own ability to work things out.

But, if there is not even this much coherence, because Pam does not own a private plane, the airlines are on strike, she is not sufficiently interested in going to California to hire a private plane, she has no reliable friend to help out, she cannot rely on any abilities of her own to work things out later, and so on, then Pam is not justified in forming the intention to be in California tomorrow.

There is no similar requirement on *desire*. It is not inconsistent both to want *A* and to want *B* while believing one cannot have both *A* and *B*. One might very well want to marry Elizabeth and also want to marry Olivia, while believing one cannot marry both. Such a conflict in one's desires would not be incoherent in the way it would be incoherent to intend to marry Elizabeth and also intend to marry Olivia while believing one cannot marry both. Nor is one in any way unjustified in having desires for things one cannot coherently imagine getting, given one's beliefs and other desires. On the other hand Pam can without any irrationality desperately desire to be in California during the airline strike without having the faintest idea how to get there. Because desires are not subject to requirements of consistency and coherence, I am inclined to suppose that changes in desires are never "part of" reasoning but can only at most "result from" reasoning (chapter 1). Here then is an important difference between desires and intentions, indicating that intentions cannot be reduced to desires.

Hopes are an intermediate case. On the one hand hopes are like intentions and beliefs in being subject to some sort of coherence constraint. It is inconsistent to hope for A and also to hope for B, while believing that at most one of A and B can occur. One cannot any more coherently hope to marry Olivia and also hope to marry Elizabeth, believing one cannot marry both, than one can coherently intend these things or believe them. On the other hand, as with desires, it seems one can be justified in hoping for something one cannot coherently imagine getting, given one's beliefs and other hopes. Pam can coherently hope to be in California tomorrow without having the faintest idea how she will get there. To be sure, she cannot coherently hope to be in California tomorrow without also hoping some way will emerge for getting there. But similarly it may be that Pam cannot coherently desire to be in California without also desiring that some way will emerge for getting there. (I am not sure about this.)

Positive Intentions Involve a Plan

If one intends to A, this intention must cohere with one's beliefs and other intentions. If one's intention is a positive intention, one must have some idea of how one's intention will lead one to A, however dim this idea may be. One must have a *plan* for A-ing. The plan does not have to be worked out in detail; one can plan to fill in details later as needed as long as it is reasonable to plan to do this, given one's other plans and beliefs. In New Jersey in May Pam can intend to be in California next September without having yet decided how she will get there, so long as she can rely on her ability to make arrangements later.

This associated plan is also something one intends. If one intends to go to the party tonight and one's plan is to get there by taxi, one intends to go to the party tonight by taxi.

In fact, as the example indicates, one's plan to accomplish what one intends is actually included in that very intention. One's intention is to do A by following such and such a plan. One intends to do A by B-ing.

Recall that, when one has a positive intention, one thinks of one's intention as responsible for one's doing as one intends. One supposes one would not do what one intends unless one intended to do it. This contrasts with a negative intention in which one makes no such supposition. One envisions a connection between a positive intention and the intended action. One envisions one's intention leading one to do A by leading one to take various intermediate steps, perhaps including additional planning when needed. To repeat, since the plan is one's means for getting *A*, what one envisions here is something one intends. One intends this connection between one's intention and one's action.

The intended connection may be relatively direct. One may simply intend to act directly when the moment arrives. Then one envisions one's intention continuing to exist until the required moment, at which point it leads one to act directly. The intended connection between present intention and later action in this case is simply that one's intention should continue to exist until the required moment, at which point it leads one to act as one intends. The intention that this should occur must cohere with one's other intentions and beliefs. One cannot coherently intend to act directly tomorrow if, for example, one is sure one will by then have forgotten what one now intends to do at that point or if one is sure one won't at that point be able to bring oneself to act in the required way.

The point applies even to the intention to do something directly now. Even in that case one has a plan, a conception of how one intends to be doing what one intends. One intends to be doing it directly. One intends that one's intention should be leading in the normal direct way to one's doing as one intends. To intend to be raising one's arm in the ordinary direct way is different from intending to be raising it by pulling with one's foot on a wire looped around a pulley. One intends a different connection in the two cases between one's intention and one's act, direct in the one case, indirect in the other.

To avoid misunderstanding, I should say that a connection between the intention to do *A* and doing *A* is "direct" in this sense when (1) if one intends to do *A*, that will lead one to do *A* and (2) the connection between intention and act is not mediated by an intention to do anything else as a means to doing *A*. Even in the case of a direct intention, the actual causal story might be complicated and might be different for different people or for the same person at different times (for example, before and after a brain operation). To intend that one should do something "in the normal direct way" is not to intend that the actual causal story be simple or that it be what it has normally been in the past.

Intentions Are Always in Part about Themselves

Since the plan associated with a positive intention includes one's having that very intention, one must intend to have that intention, intending it to lead in a certain way to one's action. A positive intention is therefore always at least somewhat complex and is always in part about itself. It is always the intention that it itself will lead in such and such a way to such and such a result (Harman 1976; Searle 1983, chap. 3). Intending to go to the party by taxi tonight is intending that this very intention will be responsible for one's taking steps to obtain a taxi which will take one to the party tonight. Intending to be raising one's arm is intending that this very intention is in the normal direct way leading one to be raising one's arm.

Various things show that a positive intention is always about itself in the sense that one intends the intention itself to lead in a certain way to a certain result. For example, what one envisions as one's means is intended. So, since one thinks of the connection between one's intention and some further result as a necessary part of one's means of accomplishing that result, that connection is intended. Furthermore, this explains why one can coherently form a positive intention to do something only if it is reasonable to envision that intention leading one to act as one intends. That is a consequence of the general coherence requirement on intention, given that one's intention to do *A* is that that very intention should lead to one's doing *A* in a certain way.

If one intends to do *A* and one's intention to do *A* leads one to do *A* but in a sufficiently different way from the way one envisioned, we are reluctant to say one does *A* intentionally, since (as we say) the result is not what one intended. To take an example from Chisholm (1966), one intends to drive across town to kill an enemy, who, however, happens to be walking past one's house as one backs out of one's driveway; one runs over the enemy, killing him instantly. We are reluctant to say one kills one's enemy intentionally in such a case, since what happened is not at all what was intended, even if one had intended to kill him by running over him! In the same way, if a gunman's intention to kill his victim makes him so nervous that he inadvertently shoots and kills his victim, we are again reluctant to say he intentionally shoots the victim (Davidson 1973), since what happened is not what he intended. The gunman intended that his intention would lead him to shoot in a more straightforward, normal simple way.

It is possible to avoid the supposition that positive intentions are always in part about themselves by supposing there are always two intentions, the intention to do *A* and the "metaintention" the first intention should lead to one's doing *A* in such and such a way. Or, to avoid a bothersome infinite regress, it could be suggested that an intention is always accompanied by a metaintention unless the first intention is itself already the metaintention that a particular intention should have a certain result. But these and other ways of escaping the self-referentiality of intentions seem contrived and pointless to me, so I continue to assume intentions are always in part about themselves.

Self-Referential Attitudes

There has always been some reluctance to suppose attitudes might be self-referential. This reluctance is probably due to the widespread view that self-reference leads to the liar paradox, discussed in chapter 2. That is a shame, since that is the wrong moral to draw from the liar paradox (whatever the right moral may be), and many interesting psychological phenomena are illuminated once we see that attitudes can be self-referential.

Let us briefly consider these points. First, recall the liar paradox. It arises for beliefs such as the belief (L) that that very belief (L) is not true. For it may seem that all instances of the following schema must be accepted:

> *Biconditional Truth Schema*   The belief that Q is true if and only if Q.

Applying this to the belief (L) (that (L) is not true), yields the result that (L) is true if and only if (L) is not true, which is logically inconsistent.

Some people have argued this shows there cannot be beliefs about themselves like (L). But it is not reasonable to suppose the correct response to the liar paradox is simply to disallow such self-referential attitudes. One can sometimes believe another person's belief is not true, and that is enough to yield a version of the liar paradox if the other person's belief happens to be that one's own belief is true. Or one might simply confuse someone else with oneself, in which case one's belief might in fact be the paradoxical belief (L). Such a belief is clearly not impossible. (See Kripke (1975) for more discussion of this point.)

The source of the liar paradox is the Biconditional Truth Schema. The paradox shows that not all instances of this schema can be accepted. No perfectly adequate account has been given as to which are the acceptable instances. For example, as Kripke (1975) remarks, it is inadequate to suggest the schema does not apply to self-referential beliefs, since there are some self-referential beliefs to which we do want to apply the schema. As I suggested in chapter 2, we cannot at this point formulate a fully adequate and rigorous theory of truth. At best we must make do with the nonrigorous theory that accepts the Biconditional Truth Schema as a defeasible principle or default assumption that holds only "other things being equal."

I mentioned that there are several phenomena that are illuminated if we suppose attitudes can be self-referential. One of course is the very phenomenon of intention which I have been discussing. Another is meaning or communication as analyzed in Grice (1957), which also

involves self-referential intentions but in a different way. To mean that
P in Grice's sense is to give some sign to an audience intending the
audience to think that *P* by virtue of their recognition (on the basis of
that sign) that one has *that very intention*. Grice himself originally states
his analysis as involving a self-referential intention in this way; but,
because of worries about what he calls "self-reflective paradox," he
goes on to restate the analysis as involving a series of intentions, each
about the preceding one. This turns out to lead to tremendous complexity
in the resulting theory. Either there are only a finite number of such
intentions, in which case counterexamples seem to arise, or there is a
vicious infinite regress of different intentions, which is absurd (see
Grice 1969). Much of this complexity is artificial and due to Grice's
refusal to stick with the original analysis and its appeal to a self-
referential intention (Harman 1974).

A related phenomenon is what Lewis (1975, p. 6) and Schiffer (1972)
call *common* or *mutual knowledge*. It is common knowledge in a group
that *P* if and only if each member of the group knows "*P* and we know
this," where "this" refers to the entire thing known. However, neither
Lewis nor Schiffer gives an analysis in this self-referential form, each
speaking instead of a series of things known: Each member of the
group knows (1) that *P*, (2) that each member of the group knows that
P, (3) that each member of the group knows that each member of the
group knows that *P*, and so on. There are various ways we might
attempt to avoid an unwelcome infinite regress here (Lewis 1969, pp.
51–56; Bennett 1976), but the most natural one is to suppose that the
members of the group have the self-referential knowledge "*P* and we
know this" (Harman 1974, 1977).

Searle (1983) gives a number of other good examples. For example,
he suggests that the visual experience of seeing a yellow station wagon
might have roughly the following content: "This very visual experience
is caused by the presence before me of a yellow station wagon" (p. 48).
And in Harman (1980) I suggest that every theoretical conclusion is in
part about itself, taking the form, "I believe this because of something
that settles it that *P*." Taking an example from Goldman (1967), on
seeing some lava at the base of a mountain, one concludes, "This was
once a volcano which erupted, giving forth this lava, which has remained
here to be seen by me, leading me to form this very belief."

But this is a digression. Let us return to the subject of intending.

Intention and Intentional Action

It is tempting to see too close a connection between doing something
intentionally and intending to do what one does. In particular, it is
tempting to accept the following principle:

Putative Principle That Intentional Acts Are Always Intended   If one acts intentionally, it follows that one intended to act in that way.

This Putative Principle is one source of the view, which I have rejected, that intentions are merely implicit in other states and in the way they cause behavior. It can initially seem quite plausible that whether an action is intentional may depend entirely on the way in which it arises from one's desires and beliefs, and then it is a simple inference to the conclusion that one's intentions must be merely implicit in such desires and beliefs. Beardsley (1978) explicitly argues in this way. Davidson (1978) reports that this line of thought lies behind what is said about intention in Davidson (1963).

I have already mentioned two reasons to reject this approach. First, in order to avoid counterexamples it is necessary to specify that the relevant desires and beliefs must lead to the resulting action in a certain way, but it seems impossible to specify the required way without mentioning one's intentions, for example, by saying an act is intentional if and only if it is a consequence of beliefs and desires in a way that one intends. Second, this approach cannot be extended to cover negative and conditional intentions or even current ongoing positive intentions to do something later.

Furthermore, the Putative Principle That Intentional Acts Are Always Intended is incorrect. In particular, things one does as foreseen consequences or side effects of what one intends to do sometimes count as intentional without being intended. Someone who foresees that his attempts to extricate himself from a tight parking spot will dent your fender may reluctantly go ahead, intentionally denting your fender in the process, without having aimed at or intended this in any way.

Such examples depend on there being a difference between a foreseen aspect of one's action that one intends as end or means and a foreseen aspect that one does not intend. We normally suppose there is such a difference. I discuss the basis of this distinction in chapter 9.

There are other more controversial examples that seem to conflict with the Putative Principle That Intentional Acts Are Always Intended. Some of these involve attempts to do something when one is not sure one will succeed. If one does succeed in such cases, it often seems more correct to say one acted intentionally than to say flatly that one intended to do what one did. A sniper who fires from a distance and hits the ambassador may be said to have killed the ambassador intentionally. But, if the sniper thought the chances were not great that he would hit the ambassador from that distance, it seems imprecise to say flatly that he intended to hit the ambassador, rather than that he intended to try. However, this is not a clear case and people disagree about it, some holding that even in that case it is quite proper to say the sniper intended to kill the ambassador. I return to this issue in the next section of this chapter.

Bratman (to appear) gives a different sort of argument, observing that there are cases in which one tries to do either A or B, believing one cannot succeed in doing both. Modifying his example, a bowler tries to roll a bowling ball in such a way that it will hit either one or the other of two pins that are separated in such a way that both cannot be hit with the ball. If the bowler hits one of the pins, we might say she hit the pin intentionally, but we cannot say that she intended to hit the pin, at least if her intentions are coherent with her beliefs, because by symmetry it would also have to be said that she intended to hit the other pin too. In that case the bowler's intentions would not have been coherent with her beliefs, because she believed that one could not hit both, and it is incoherent to intend A and intend B while believing one cannot do both.

However, matters are complicated by the fact that judgments about whether an act is intentional or intended are sensitive to context or emphasis. We would not say that the bowler intentionally hit the left pin *rather than the right pin* and so could deny that the bowler intentionally hit the *left* pin, with emphasis on "left." Similarly, it is possible that, when we deny that the bowler intended to hit the left pin, we interpret this to be understood as implying "rather than the right pin." In that case, it might be acceptable to say that the bowler intended to hit the left pin if no such contrast is implied. Perhaps, strictly, the bowler's hitting the left pin is neither intended nor intentional, although loosely it can be said to be both intended and intentional.

I do not know under what conditions it is true or appropriate to say someone does something intentionally, but the conditions of intentional action seem to have only a loose relation to the conditions of intended action. In particular, it is clear that foreseen consequences of what one does can be intentional without having been intended. So, the Putative Principle That Intentional Acts Are Always Intended is incorrect.

Intention and Belief

It is quite controversial whether intending to do something always involves believing one will do it. To some extent this is because it is easy to confuse this question with others, such as whether doing something intentionally always involves believing one will do it. And to some extent the controversy depends on admitting different standards for believing than for intending. But even after all confusions and mistakes are cleared up, there still seem to be irresolvable disputes over certain examples. I am almost tempted to think different people mean different things by the key terms here, although I feel that such a hypothesis is always a last resort.

I should say that, in addition to this linguistic question concerning how we use the words "intend" and "intention," there is also a more substantive question about the extent to which one can even try to do things without believing one will succeed. I argue in chapter 9 that there are severe limits on the extent to which one can do this. At this point I am concerned with the purely verbal issue.

Let me begin by mentioning phenomena which suggest that intending to do something does involve believing one will do it. First, there is the point mentioned already that if one tries to do something thinking the chances of success are low, then it can seem incorrect to say one intends to succeed. For example, in playing golf, Jane tries to sink a long and difficult putt. Compare saying that Jane intends to sink the putt with saying she intends to try to sink it, or hopes to sink it. The former remark, that Jane intends to sink the putt, seems to attribute a confidence to her that the latter remarks do not.

Suppose Jane sinks the putt to everyone's surprise, including her own, and then says, "That is what I intended." That seems to involve a certain amount of bragging that is not involved in saying, "That is what I was trying to do" or "That is what I was hoping to do." It suggests she knew or was confident she would sink the putt. Such implications of a statement about what someone intends would be accounted for by the principle that intending to do something involves believing one will do it.

I agree that it would be more reasonable for Jane to say she intended to sink the putt given certain contexts. For example, suppose it is suggested that, because of her lack of skill, Jane was playing conservatively, not trying to sink the ball on this shot but just trying to put the ball close enough to the cup to sink it on the next shot. But, the suggestion continues, Jane accidentally hit the ball too hard and so inadvertently sank the putt. If Jane replies, "No, I intended to sink the putt on this shot," that does not seem to be a case of bragging. (Here I am indebted to Robert Stalnaker.)

But even in a case like this it would be more honest for Jane to say, "No, I was trying to sink the putt on this shot." Her remark that she intended to sink the putt does not sound like bragging when it is contrasted with the remark that she was only trying to get near the hole, but it does sound like bragging when contrasted with the more accurate remark that she was trying to sink the putt on this shot. So, there is still support here for the principle that intending to do something involves believing one will do it, although delicate and controversial questions of language are involved.

Let me turn now to apparent considerations on the other side, which seem to me to be based on some sort of error. First, it might be said that, if Jane sinks the putt, she sinks the putt intentionally and so must have intended to sink the putt. But this argument fails. For one thing it is quite controversial whether Jane can be properly said to have intentionally sunk the putt in a case like this. People disagree about the case. To me, this also sounds like bragging on her behalf.

We have already considered a better case of this sort, in which a sniper who is not confident of success shoots at the ambassador. When he succeeds, we can say he intentionally shoots the ambassador. (The difference between this case and Jane's putting case may reflect an asymmetry in our willingness to praise and blame people. Perhaps we are more inclined to count the sniper as having intentionally shot the ambassador, because we are inclined to blame the sniper for the ambassador's death, whereas we are less inclined to count Jane as having intentionally sunk the putt, because we are reluctant to praise her for this, preferring to attribute her success to luck rather than her skill at putting.) However, the fact that the sniper shoots the ambassador intentionally does not show that the sniper intends to shoot the ambassador. The Putative Principle That Intentional Acts Are Always Intended is false. And, as I have already remarked, the example itself is controversial. It is controversial whether the sniper flatly intends to shoot the ambassador in a situation like this. So the example cannot be used without begging the question to argue that one can intend to do something without believing one will do it.

Another inconclusive argument for doubting that intending to do something implies believing one will do it is that one can intend to do something without being sure one will succeed. Pam can intend to fly from New Jersey to California tomorrow even though she realizes there are all sorts of things that might keep her from doing this.

But this does not show what it is supposed to show. Just as one can intend to do something without being sure of success, one can believe something without being sure the belief is true. For example, Pam may believe she will fly to California tomorrow without being sure she will get there. So, Pam's intending to fly to California tomorrow can involve believing she will fly to California tomorrow even if she is not sure she will get there.

Similarly, although it is true that "I intend to do A" is a more tentative remark than saying simply, "I will do A," that does not show intending to do A can occur without believing one will do A. "I believe I will do A" is also a more tentative remark than "I will do A," but that does not show believing one will do *A* can occur without believing one will do *A*! (Here I am indebted to Stuart Hampshire.)

Another argument against the implication from intending to believing might be based on the thought that intention often involves *determination* to do something rather than belief in success. A tennis player who wants to play better is well advised to intend to win, but this involves nothing more than being determined to win, whether or not there are sufficient grounds to believe he or she will in fact win. But again this is inconclusive. The relevant sort of determination seems to me to require that the player get him- or herself to *believe* he or she will win, whether or not there are sufficient theoretical grounds to believe this! So, all this shows is that one can have a kind of practical justification for trying to get oneself to believe one will win in certain cases in which this belief is not warranted by the evidence.

I see no compelling reason to reject the claim that intending to do something involves believing one will do it. But, as I have already remarked, the point remains controversial. Even after all mistakes and confusions are eliminated, people still seem to disagree about the correct way of describing certain cases. And maybe this shows people use the key terms differently, although I don't like to suggest that.

Intending, Acting with an Intention, and Aiming

In the absence of full belief it is often easier to say or believe someone acts "with the intention" of doing *A* than to say he or she acts "intending" to do *A*. In the case of Jane's surprisingly successful putt, it is clearer that Jane hit the ball "with the intention" of sinking the putt than that she hit the ball intending to sink the putt.

Sometimes the noun "intention" seems to be synonymous with the "aim." Jane's aim was to sink the putt; that was her intention. But the verb "intend" seems less close in meaning to the verb "aim" for reasons that are not clear to me. It is clear that Jane aimed at sinking the putt, but it is far from clear that she intended to sink it. Similarly, although it is clear that she intended to *try* to sink the putt, it is less clear that she *aimed* at trying to sink it.

Furthermore, negative intentions are not aims. One can have the intention of staying home tonight without having that as one's aim. That is one's aim only if one supposes one needs to aim at it in order to achieve it; but then the intention is positive rather than negative. Since there does not seem to be the same contrast between "intend" and "intention" for negative intentions as for positive intentions, it is possible that there is a distinct use of the word "intention" in which it is synonymous with "aim" and another use in which one has an intention to do something only if one intends to do it. If so, then, in the first sense, one can have the intention (aim) of doing A without the belief that one will do A, whereas in the second sense, one can have the intention of doing A only if one has the belief that one will do A.

Committing the Will

Intention seems to involve a kind of commitment of the will. Perhaps what Davidson (1978) calls an all-out evaluative judgment is best understood instead as expressing this sort of commitment of the will. As we have seen, Davidson's proposal suggests the possibility of all-out evaluative judgments of this sort concerning nonactions, such as things one hopes will happen without intending to bring them about. And this suggests that hoping may involve the same sort of commitment of the will that is involved in intending.

One aspect of commitment involved in intending is that one's intentions must be coherent with each other and with one's beliefs. Since one's hopes are subject to the same requirement of coherence, this is some confirmation of the idea that hoping and intending have in common a certain commitment of the will. One's desires, which involve no such commitment, are not subject to this requirement.

On the other hand one's beliefs are subject to a requirement of coherence which indicates they involve a kind of commitment, but this is not a commitment of the will of the sort that intention, and maybe hoping, involve.

Although hoping and intending may both involve commitment of the will, it seems incorrect to say one always hopes one's intentions will succeed. If one arbitrarily selects one from several apples in a bowl, it would be incorrect to say one *hopes* to take that apple but not incorrect to say one *intends* to take it. Still, one's will is committed to that apple, even though the commitment is a trivial one which is easily deflected.

Grice (1972) suggests that, if one's will is committed to P and one knows one can bring about P, one will be inclined to do so. This is often so, but (as Claudia Mills has pointed out to me) it is not always so if hoping involves the relevant sort of commitment of the will. One might hope P will happen without one's own agency; for example, one hopes that one's medical test results do not indicate any serious illness.

If hoping and intending involve the same sort of commitment of the will, how do they differ? It is not just that intending to A involves believing one will A and that hoping to A does not involve such a belief. If one hopes to sneeze and then becomes convinced one will sneeze, that is not yet to intend to sneeze.

One suggestion would be that intending is self-referential in a way that hoping is not. In this view, to intend or aim to A is to have one's will committed to doing A as an upshot of having that very commitment, or (to allow for negative intentions) to have one's will committed to that very commitment's settling it that one will do A. If this works, it is an elegant solution, but does it work? Can't one hope that P will occur because of that very hope without having any intention or aim of bringing about P? A person might think it possible that God gives eternal life to those who hope for it. Such a person might then hope that that very hope will give him or her eternal life. Does he or she thereby intend to have or aim at having eternal life? It would seem not to me, although I am not sure. Perhaps this shows that there is a different sort of commitment of the will involved in hoping and in intending or aiming.

On the other hand suppose a person becomes convinced that God gives eternal life to those who hope for it. Then the person might hope that this very hope will give him or her eternal life, except that his or her attitude is more than hope. The person now believes the hope will give him or her eternal life, but hope is appropriate only where one does not yet believe. Indeed, I find it hard to distinguish the person's resulting attitude from *opting* for eternal life in a sense which involves intention. In this case, intention seems to require not only the appropriate sort of self-referential commitment of the will but also belief that one will do what one is committed to doing.

Summary

Practical reasoning revises one's intentions, so in this chapter I have tried to bring out some of the features of intending to do something. My main point has been that intentions are not merely implicit in beliefs and desires but are distinctive attitudes that play a special role in thought and action. It has proved important to see that not all intentions are positive intentions, leading one to do as one intends. There are negative and conditional intentions too. Intentions of all sorts are like beliefs and unlike desires in being subject to requirements of consistency and coherence. Intentions always in part concern themselves; in particular, positive intentions always involve plans concerning how they are to be realized. The relation between intention and intentional action is obscure; and it is useful to observe that one can intentionally do something without having intended to do it. Intending to do something may involve believing one will do it; familiar arguments to the contrary are not conclusive, and the point remains controversial. Finally, intention involves a distinctive sort of commitment of the will and it is unclear whether hoping involves the same sort of commitment.

Chapter 9
Intended and Merely Foreseen Consequences

In a typical intentional action, one has an end E which one intends to achieve by means M, possibly foreseeing side effects S of M and consequences C of E:

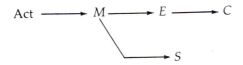

Normally, we suppose that, although M and E are intended, S and C need not be intended but might be merely foreseen.

For example, an assassin intends to kill the Prime Minister by shooting her with a rifle from ambush. The assassin foresees this will make a loud noise, heat the barrel of the rifle, and cause the Prime Minister to fall out of her seat. We would normally suppose the assassin intends the pulling of the trigger and the shooting and killing of the Prime Minister without necessarily intending the loud noise, the heating of the barrel of the gun, or the Prime Minister's fall from her seat.

Similarly, an army commander intends to kill the enemy hidden in a village by bombing the village, realizing this will as a side effect also kill noncombatants in the village, also realizing that, as a consequence of the death of the enemy soldiers, their surviving friends and relatives will be made unhappy. We would normally suppose this is compatible with the army commander's not intending either the deaths of the noncombatants or the unhappiness of the relatives of the enemy soldiers.

Again, Albert intends to improve the appearance of his lawn by cutting the grass with his power lawn mower, realizing this will release some fumes into the air and irritate Betty across the street, who wants her lawn to be the best-looking lawn on the block. We would normally think there is no need to assume Albert intends either the fumes or the irritation to Betty.

A Holistic Challenge

On reflection it is not obvious that the way we ordinarily think about these cases is correct. When one decides what to do, one should do so in the awareness that one's decision will have many aspects. One is therefore committed to accepting the whole story, including means, ends, side effects, and consequences. Whether one should make that decision depends not only on the value of accomplishing one's end but also on the value or disvalue of the rest of this story. That can make it seem misleading to say that only some parts of the story are intended, others merely foreseen.

For example, in deciding whether to take a particular medicine to relieve one's back pain, one should obviously consider not only the question whether taking the medicine is an effective means to one's immediate end, relief of back pain, but also whether the medicine might have undesirable side effects, such as reduced hearing in the future. When one decides whether to take the drug, one should consider one's assessment of the whole story. It is irrational to think only of the question whether taking the drug will be an effective means, ignoring possible side effects.

Similarly, the army commander must take into account the side effects of bombing the village. The fact that the bombing will kill noncombatants as well as enemy soldiers affects its desirability. It would be wrong to ignore that side effect.

These reflections suggest what I call a holistic view of decisions. In a holistic view, when one decides what to do, one must consider all foreseeable effects, consequences, and other aspects of one's decision and must evaluate them as a total package. Good or bad side effects and consequences affect the desirability of one's decision in exactly the way that good or bad ends or means do.

Once this much is accepted, it becomes difficult to see how there could be a real distinction between what one intends and what one merely foresees as consequences and side effects of one's action, because it is natural to suppose that (A) one's intention comprises the conclusion one reaches as the result of practical reasoning. But in a holistic view of practical reasoning, (B) one's conclusion should include the acceptance of everything one knows about one's action and its foreseen side effects and consequences just as much as a certain end and means. Supposition (A) is hard to reject, because if (A) is not accepted it is extremely difficult to see what the connection could be between one's intentions and one's practical conclusions. Supposition (B) is simply holism. Together, (A) and (B) imply that all foreseen aspects of one's decision, including side effects and consequences, should be as much a part of one's intention as one's end and means are. So, it is hard to accept holism without supposing we should abandon our ordinary view that foreseen consequences and side effects are not intended in the way that our ends and means are. Without considering what alternatives there might be to this, I simply assume that (A) is so in what follows and consider only that version of holism which holds that all foreseen aspects of one's action are intended.

The Issue Joined

A natural objection to holism is that, even though side effects and foreseen consequences are *potentially* relevant, they are not always actually relevant. There often is the following difference between one's means M and end E on the one hand and a side effect S or foreseen consequence C on the other hand: It is the thought of E and M that provides one's reason for acting as one does. One's knowledge that one's act will also have the side effect S and the consequence C plays no role in one's deciding to act in that way. Therefore M and E are part of what one intends in a way that S and C are not.

This objection accepts (A), agreeing that one's intention can be identified with one's practical conclusion, but rejects (B), with its claim that one's practical conclusion should include the acceptance of foreseen side effects and consequences in the same way that it includes the acceptance of means and end.

The holists' reply to this objection is to deny that one's awareness of side effects S and consequences C should ever fail to be part of one's reason for acting as one does. One's reason should always include an assessment of all aspects of the action, including an assessment of the desirability of side effects and consequences as much as it includes an assessment of the desirability of ends and means. There will always be a different possible side effect S_1 or consequence C_1 such that, if one had thought it would result rather than S and C, one should not have acted in the way one acted. One's aim in doing something is to bring about this relatively desirable set of consequences, including relatively neutral S or C as opposed to undesirable S_1 or C_1.

Holism and Double Effect

The holistic thesis, that all foreseen aspects of an act are intended, including foreseen side effects and consequences, has an obvious bearing on issues in moral philosophy relating to the Catholic Doctrine of Double Effect. This doctrine presupposes that foreseen consequences are not always intended. In the Catholic view there are some things one absolutely must not intend, for example the killing of an innocent and nonthreatening person. These things must never be one's end or one's means to some end, although by the Doctrine of Double Effect they may be allowed in extreme circumstances as foreseen but unintended side effects or consequences. For example, in war the intended killing of noncombatants as a means to weaken the enemy's will is absolutely forbidden, whereas the unintended but foreseen killing of a few noncombatants in the course of bombing enemy soldiers might under certain circumstances be allowed.

One can accept a version of the doctrine of Double Effect even if one does not agree that the intended killing of innocent people is always forbidden no matter what, even to save the world. It is enough to think, for example, that it might sometimes be wrong to aim at the death of noncombatants even if it would not be wrong to kill the same number of noncombatants in a similar way but as a mere side effect of a direct attack aimed solely at enemy soldiers. On a smaller scale one might suppose it would be wrong of Albert to cut his grass with the specific intention of making Betty unhappy, even though it would not be wrong of Albert to cut his grass to improve the appearance of his lawn if he merely foresees without intending that this will make Betty unhappy.

To take an example from Foot (1967), most people think it is one thing to refuse to contribute to charities aimed at preventing starvation because one prefers to use the money instead on oneself; it is quite another to refrain from contributing on the grounds that the resulting deaths will provide bodies for medical researchers. Most people think refraining for this latter reason is much worse, even though medical progress is a nobler end than mere self-interest, because the deaths from starvation are one's *means* to this nobler end and not merely a foreseen but unintended consequence of spending one's money on oneself.

Holism, which leans toward consequentialism in moral philosophy, obviously clashes with the principle of Double Effect. Holists think the distinction invoked by defenders of Double Effect is irrational, perhaps even immoral.

I am not really interested in a full-scale discussion of Double Effect. I have mentioned it only to help bring out part of what is involved in the question of holism. In mentioning Double Effect, I do not mean to express either approval or disapproval. In particular, I do not mean to suggest that the plausibility of (at least a weak version of) Double Effect is an objection to holism. Holists can agree that the distinction between intended and merely foreseen consequences of an act is initially plausible. Their claim is not that this is implausible initially but rather that the distinction does not survive careful serious reflection.

Furthermore, I do not wish to suggest that holism can be rejected only by those who accept Double Effect. It may be possible to distinguish intended ends and means from merely foreseen side effects and consequences without accepting Double Effect. There may be objections to Double Effect that are not objections to the distinction between intended and merely foreseen consequences. It is important not to treat these ideas as equivalent.

Holistic Decision Making with Perfect Information

I now want to explore holism in greater detail. Holism is based on a view about how one ought to make decisions. To take the simplest case, suppose one is deciding between two courses of action, A and B, knowing everything about each act and its consequences. Then holism recommends comparing all aspects of A and its consequences to all aspects of B and its consequences in order to determine which total package yields the most desirable overall result. What one should decide on is the total package and one should then act in order to bring about that whole package. So in this view there should be no principled distinction between intended and merely foreseen parts of this package.

Brandt (1979), accepting a version of holism, observes that in making such a decision it is important to get all relevant considerations clearly and vividly in mind. Otherwise some factors will probably be overrated and others ignored or underrated. But this points to a problem. There are severe limits on the number of things a person can have vividly in mind (Miller 1956). In practice, some method must be used to simplify any problem involving more than six or seven distinct factors.

Brandt mentions a method of simplification which was recommended by Benjamin Franklin (1817). The idea is to make two lists, a list of the relevant factors favoring A and a list of the factors favoring B. Then one should try to find factors on list A that can be equated with factors on list B. When this is done, one is to strike out the equivalent sets of factors, then try again with the remaining factors, continuing until the problem has been simplified to the point at which it leaves a comparison whose elements can be placed vividly in one's mind at the same time.

Although this method can be useful, it does not always yield a definite answer. Sometimes, one gets down to things that are difficult to compare, such as relief from severe pain with some hearing loss *versus* the pain but no hearing loss, or a career as an engineer *versus* a career as a lawyer.

Such hard decisions might be easier if a certain form of egoistic hedonism were correct. In this view one's ultimate goal is always one's own happiness, measured in terms of pleasure and pain, where amounts of pleasure and pain are always comparable, any possible pain can always be balanced by a corresponding possible pleasure, and vice versa, and perhaps temporal considerations are irrelevant so that pain now, pleasure later is equivalent to pleasure now, pain later. Then, in choosing between becoming an engineer and becoming a lawyer, the issue becomes which choice will make one happier in the long run— and that is something one will know if one has perfect information about the consequences of one's choice.

Less Than Perfect Knowledge

So far I have been considering what holism says about the case in which one is deciding between *A* and *B* with perfect knowledge of all aspects of these choices. Of course, in practice, one will never know *all* aspects. Indeed, such perfect knowledge would include the knowledge of which act is better, and there would be no decision problem left! If the decision problem has not been solved already, there cannot be absolutely *perfect* knowledge of all aspects of the actions. The difficulties I have been discussing do not actually arise if there is really perfect knowledge!

Is it enough to know the *difference in consequences* between *A* and *B*? It depends on how we conceive this "difference." Thinking of things one way, we find that the relative desirability of *A* and *B* may depend not only on the difference between them but also on the constant possibly unknown context that is common to both acts. For example, the army commander knows that the difference between bombing the village and not bombing it is that in the former case a certain number of enemy and noncombatants are killed, a certain number of bombs are exploded, and so much airplane fuel is used, whereas in the latter case none of this happens. It is also relevant whether or not the war has already ended, something the commander may not know. But, in this way of looking at things, that is not part of the *difference in consequences* between *A* and *B*, since whether or not the war has already ended is a constant factor which remains the same no matter which course of action the commander takes.

Similarly, in deciding whether to invest in gold or diamonds, Judy may know that in the former case she will have gold, in the latter case diamonds, but she may not know what the relative value of gold and diamonds will be five years from now. This constant factor is relevant to her decision. So it is not enough to know the *differences in consequences* between A and B if they are conceived in this way.

However, there is another way of looking at things. In this view the differences in consequences are not fully known. The army commander does not know whether the bombing will contribute to the defeat of the enemy; so he does not know whether such a contribution distinguishes bombing from not bombing the village. Judy does not know which investment, gold or diamonds, will be worth more in five years; so she does not know what the difference between A and B is as regards its contribution to the value of her investment in five years.

But, if this sort of thing counts as a difference in consequences, then saying one must know all the differences in consequences is not much better than saying one must know all aspects of the act. Given *any* common aspect C of both A and B, there is a corresponding difference in consequences between A and B, since A has the consequence that A & C is true, a consequence which B does not have, whereas B has the consequence that B & C is true, a consequence that A does not have. So to say one has to know all the differences in consequences is not to say something appreciably weaker than that one has to know all aspects of the act. Just as one never knows all aspects of the act, one never knows all the differences in consequences in this sense.

Again, egoistic hedonism would simplify the problem. All one would need to know is which act will give one more overall happiness in the long run. But things are more complicated if one has several distinct ultimate ends. In that case perhaps it is enough to know, for each of the acts one is deciding between, how much that act would give one of each of one's ultimate ends. If one has only a few ultimate ends, one might be able to get that information vividly in mind so that one could balance the different considerations against each other and reach an overall decision.

It would *not* be enough to know the *differences* between what A and B give one concerning each end if one has several ends, since comparative desirabilities may depend on the amounts that are constant from act to act. For example, suppose one values both pleasure and knowledge and these can be measured. Suppose acts A, B, C, and D would have the following outcomes:

A 4 units of pleasure, 8 units of knowledge.
B 2 units of pleasure, 10 units of knowledge.
C 10 units of pleasure, 2 units of knowledge.
D 8 units of pleasure, 4 units of knowledge.

Then one might prefer A to B without preferring C to D even though the *differences* between what A and B give one of the things one ultimately values are the same as the differences between what C and D give.

Probability

It might be said one can never know for certain what the relevant consequences of one's acts will be. There is always the possibility, however remote, that the difference between A and B is the difference between life as usual and utter ruin.

In the absence of complete knowledge of relevant consequences, one might try to take probabilities into account and consider the expected utility of each possible act. From this perspective, the reason why one can normally disregard the possibility that an act A will lead to total ruin is that the probability of this is usually so low that this possibility does not affect significantly the total expected utility of A.

How might one discover expected utilities? If egoistic hedonism were true and happiness were measurable, the thing to do would be to consider the various possible outcomes of a given act, take the total happiness involved in each outcome times the probability of that outcome, and then sum these products to get the expected utility of the act.

Things are not so simple if egoistic hedonism is not assumed. One must in some more complicated way determine the utilities of the various possible outcomes, multiply these utilities by the probabilities of the outcomes, and sum these products. However, there are serious obstacles to calculating expected utility in this way.

First, how is one to determine the utilities of the possible outcomes? The standard method for determining these utilities supposes one already knows the preferences one has among various gambles (Ramsey 1931; von Neumann and Morgenstern 1944). But one's present problem is exactly that of choosing which of two gambles one prefers! Does one prefer the A gamble with its possible outcomes, each with an associated probability, or the B gamble with its possible outcomes, each with its associated probability? The trouble is that, in order to solve one's present problem by appeal to expected utility, one must already have solved similar problems directly without appeal to expected utility. How does one ever get started?

Second, even if one were somehow given these utilities, there would be the further problem of determining the relevant probabilities. If one knew appropriate relative frequencies, one could use them to estimate probabilities, but usually such information is not available. One might use one's own "degrees of belief" in various possible outcomes, but how does one determine what one's degrees of belief are? There is a problem here analogous to that which arises for utility. In standard developments of the theory of subjective probability, it is observed that degrees of belief can be deduced from information about preferences (Jeffrey 1983) if one is consistent. More precisely, a complete set of preferences determines subjective probabilities and utilities up to a linear transformation. If the utilities are fixed, then the probabilities are completely determined. But deducing degrees of belief from preferences is no help if one is trying to discover probabilities in order to determine one's preferences.

Perhaps holism's advice in the present case reduces to this:

> One should try to get all one's evidence vividly in mind, vividly consider how this evidence might be related to various possible outcomes of the acts one is deciding between, and see what tendency one has to favor each of these acts.

But if this is the sum total of holism's advice, holism merely says to consider everything carefully before deciding, without really telling how to decide.

A further complication is that one is not normally choosing between only two actions. One might do any of indefinitely many things. Holism requires considering all possible available actions and all their possible consequences also. Obviously, if one really had to go through all of that in order to decide what to do, one would end up never doing anything.

It might be suggested one does not have to do everything simultaneously. One can try to start with a small assignment of probabilities and utilities, extending and adjusting this assignment as time goes by, trying to keep the assignment consistent as one extends it, updating probabilities and utilities in the light of new information, changes in one's desires due to bodily conditions, and so on.

But even this is something one cannot actually do. It is not just that people do not deal easily with probabilities (Kahneman et al. 1982; Nisbett and Ross 1980). As we saw in chapter 3, there is even a theoretical obstacle to extensive use of explicit probabilities, since the consistent updating of probabilities has a complexity that is in general an exponential function of the number of atomic propositions involved.

Strategies

The best that can be hoped for are procedures that can be used without extensive reflection, methods that yield satisfactory results most of the time. There might also be an alarm system of some sort to alert one to occasions on which more reflection is needed or is likely to pay off, and one must have methods for dealing with these more complex occasions as well.

In order to discover what one's methods for reaching decisions are, we need to consider how in fact one actually goes about deciding what to do. And it would seem that one's decisions depend on one's beliefs, one's values and desires, and one's prior plans and intentions.

As for one's beliefs, I have already noted that one does not assign probabilities to possible outcomes in any very extensive way. Indeed, a finite creature simply cannot make extensive use of probabilities. So, one believes things for the most part in a yes/no way, modifying one's beliefs as a result of perception and reasoning. These modifications always involve small changes in only a few beliefs and do not involve the extensive updating required in a probabilistic approach.

Similarly, although there are various things one wants and values, one does not assign a precise utility to such things. One's values and wants change as a result of reflection and changes in one's bodily state. But these are small-scale changes and not the extensive changes that must occur in a probability-based system.

Also, one has various current plans and intentions. These constrain one's further practical thinking in the way that prior beliefs constrain one's theoretical thinking. Practical thinking extends and sometimes modifies one's antecedent intentions in the light of one's beliefs, desires, and values.

Furthermore, I hypothesize that many of one's decisions are of necessity what we might call *simple decisions*. These arise when one finds oneself with a salient end E and one recognizes a salient means M that will get one E. In a simple case, one does not consider whether there might be some other means to E or some other end distinct from E that one might now obtain, and one disregards any other consequences of one's act. One simply forms the intention of getting E by doing M.

When there are two salient means, one arbitrarily chooses between them, unless one of the means is obviously better than the other. If there are two salient ends and possible means clearly available to obtain either, one tries to obtain both, arbitrarily choosing an order in which to attempt this, unless one order is obviously preferable. When there are two competing ends, only one of which can be obtained, one makes an arbitrary choice, again unless one of the ends is obviously better than the other.

So, to repeat, in a simple case one forms the intention of getting E by doing M without thinking about side effects. If one happens to *notice* side effects or consequences, that does not by itself normally influence one's decision.

All this is so unless there is something that sets off an "alarm"—and even then, one merely checks to see whether the alarming consideration is sufficient to lead one not to make the decision one would otherwise make.

The basic idea, then, is to try to keep things simple. One tries to limit oneself to considering a single way of obtaining a single end. If there is a salient complication, either a sufficiently unhappy side effect or consequence or a possibly better course of action, then one tries to determine whether this is sufficient to overcome one's reason for doing the simple action. If it is not sufficient to overcome that reason, one simply disregards the complication. If it is sufficient to complicate the situation, then one does not do the simple action. At this point the complication may or may not suggest a different, possibly more complex end one might achieve, together with an available means. If it does, one starts over with that as one's end and means, going ahead as long as no alarm goes off in that case.

The rationale for this way of proceeding lies in its cost-effectiveness. I suggest that it is a workable system that yields satisfactory results most of the time. However, this can only be demonstrated by further investigation of this approach. It may be that defeasibility theories of practical reasoning (e.g., Raz 1975) shed some light here, but I am not sure.

Intended and Merely Foreseen Consequences Again

Recall the structure of a typical action with ends, means, side effects, and consequences:

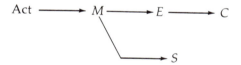

We are normally inclined to think S and C need not be intended in the way M and E are intended. We are now in a position to see how this could be so.

In a simple decision, S and C do not figure in one's practical thinking at all. After (or while or even before) deciding to achieve E by doing M, one may notice that M will lead to S and that E will lead to C, but one's noticing this occurs as part of a theoretical conclusion, not as part of a practical conclusion. One's acceptance of S and C is not part of one's acceptance of one's intention but is merely something one believes.

That explains why S and C might not be intended. However, it does not yet explain the difference between these merely foreseen consequences and the intended M and E. Why must M and E be intended?

Well, first of all, M has to be intended, because in the usual case, anyway, one won't get E unless one gets M, and one won't get M unless one aims at or intends to get M.

But then why does E have to be intended? One does not have to intend to get E in order to get it; intending to get M is sufficient. So, why not just intend to get M?

The answer seems to be this. One starts out with a desire for E, not a desire for M. One's desire for E gives one a reason to intend to get E if there is some way to manage it. Seeing that M will get one E gives one a reason to intend to get E by getting M. One has no reason to form the intention of getting M except as part of the intention of getting E. One cannot rationally intend M except as part of intending E.

Why not? Why can't this happen? One wants E. One sees that M would be a means to E. This leads one to want M, which leads one to intend M. E is not intended but is merely a foreseen, if welcome, consequence of doing what one intends. This seems absurd, but what rules it out? Why can't one's desire for M give one a reason to intend M even if one does not intend E?

The answer, I suppose, is that there is an important distinction between *ultimate* desires and merely *instrumental* desires. One's desire for E is an ultimate desire (in this context); one's desire for M is merely instrumental, because it depends on one's belief that M is instrumental in getting E. If one were to come to think M would not be instrumental in that way, one should no longer want M. Only an ultimate desire can give one a reason to form an intention. One's reason to intend M derives, then, not from an instrumental desire for M but from an ultimate desire for E, given the thought that M will get one E.

Why do only ultimate desires count in this way? Because it is important to distinguish ends from means. It would be bad if alternative means to an end were treated in the same way as alternative ends. In the case of alternative ends, what one normally does is to try to obtain both ends through scheduling. Doing this would be silly for alternative means to a given end. It would be silly to pursue both means in sequence. Clearly, the rational thing is to choose a particular means and disregard the other.

Similarly, in more complex cases in which different courses of action have different advantages, it is a point in favor of a course of action that it would satisfy more desires than another, at least if these desires are the same in strength and would be satisfied to the same extent. But this is true only if the desires are ultimate desires. It would be silly to prefer *B* to *A* as a means of getting *E* just because *B* but not *A* achieves *E* indirectly, therefore gratifying several instrumental desires, as in the following schema:

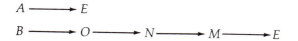

Here *A* gratifies only the desire for *E*, whereas *B* gratifies the desire for *M* as a means to *E*, *N* as a means to *M*, and *O* as a means to *N*. To treat this as a reason to prefer *B* to *A* leads to an irrational tendency toward complex ways and away from simple ways of satisfying one's desires.

It follows that even in the simple case one's intention is complex. One does not merely intend *E*, nor does one merely intend *M*. One intends to get *E* by getting *M*. More precisely, as I have argued in chapter 8, one intends that this very intention will result in one's getting *M*, which will result in one's getting *E*.

But to say one's intentions are complex in this way is not to accept holism. The preceding argument shows that one's intentions combine ends and means. There is no analogous argument for the claim that they must also include foreseen side effects and other consequences.

I have suggested that, if one notices side effects and consequences in the simple case, one notices them as the result of theoretical rather than practical reasoning, so they represent merely something one foresees as opposed to something one intends. It might be suggested further that these *cannot* be intended, because of the following putative principle:

Putative Principle That Prediction Excludes Intention   One cannot form the intention of doing something one can predict one will do whether one has that intention or not.

But this Putative Principle is not correct!

To see that it is not, consider the following example, suggested by Stuart Hampshire. Sandra is hammering nails into the floor in anticipation of the arrival in an hour of someone who is going to sand the floors. Sandra absolutely must get the nails hammered in before the sander arrives. Suddenly Sandra notices that the noise of her hammering is quite annoying to Peter. This does not sadden her. In fact, she is delighted, since she wants very much to annoy Peter. Now consider the following question. In hammering more, does Sandra *intend* to annoy Peter or is this merely a foreseen but welcome side effect?

According to the Putative Principle That Prediction Excludes Intention, Sandra cannot possibly *intend* to annoy Peter under these conditions, because she takes it to be already settled that she is going to annoy him whether she forms that intention or not. She takes this to be already settled, because she must hammer in the nails before the sander arrives and that hammering will inevitably annoy Peter.

However, it seems clear that Sandra might very well form the intention of annoying Peter under these conditions. Sandra has acquired a new reason to hammer and can surely end up hammering both for her old reason and for her new reason; she acts from two different intentions. The situation is not unlike a case in which one has two different sorts of reasons for a given belief and one believes it for both reasons. So the Putative Principle That Prediction Excludes Intention is wrong.

On the other hand Sandra might not in this circumstance intend to be annoying to Peter. That might be merely a welcome foreseen consequence of what she is doing. So this is not an argument for holism.

Intermediate Means

So far I have considered only cases in which there is a single means leading directly to an end. But often there is a series of connected intermediate means:

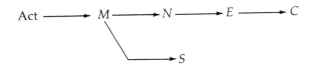

Here, M is conceived of as an indirect means to E via N. I have suggested reasons for thinking M, and E must be intended in a case like this, but what about N? Must N be intended?

We can distinguish various possibilities here. First, it may be that bringing about M merely puts one into a position to bring about E by bringing about N. In that case, one will have to intend N in order to get E. Second, it may be that one has to check to make sure that M really is bringing about N, being ready to intervene or adjust one's action if necessary. In that case, too, one will have an intention to ensure the occurrence of N.

Many, perhaps most, cases of intermediate means are of the first or second sort. But there seem to be other cases as well. Suppose one conceives the relation between M, N, and E on the model row of falling dominoes, so that having brought about M, one needs to do nothing else but wait as M brings about N and N brings about E. Then it isn't clear to me whether one needs to intend N.

It is *possible* that one intends N, since it is possible that one's practical thinking begins with the thought of bringing about E, then notes this can be done by bringing about N, and finally notes this can be done by bringing about M, so that one forms the intention of bringing about E by bringing about N, doing that by bringing about M.

But what about a case in which one starts with the thought of E and notes that one can bring about E by bringing about M, without paying particular attention to the way this works, via N, although one in fact knows that is how M will produce E? In that case I see no compelling reason to suppose N must be part of one's practical conclusion, and so no compelling reason to suppose N must be intended.

I began by suggesting that we normally suppose means have to be intended in a way that side effects and consequences do not. But I am not sure we do normally suppose this for intermediate means conceived of as this falling domino sort. I am inclined to think that knowing how the machinery works does not automatically give one intentions about the intermediate stages any more than knowing how one moves one's arm automatically gives one intentions to contract one's muscles when one raises one's arm. It seems to me one can use one's dishwasher to wash the dishes without intending the various operations of the dishwasher even if one knows what these operations are. Similarly, it seems to me one can intend to ride a bicycle up a hill without having any intention about how the chain and sprockets connect, even though one understands this is how the pedals drive the wheel.

If this is right it raises a complication for the interpretation of Double Effect. Should we interpret this doctrine as the view that it can be worse to *intend* evil than merely to foresee it? Or should we interpret the doctrine as the view that it can be worse to bring about evil as a means to one's end than as a side effect? These possibilities have to be distinguished if evil means can be known but nonintended. (When I reflect with this in mind on some of the examples already considered— the bombing of civilian populations in order to weaken an enemy's will or not giving to certain charities in order not to diminish the supply of bodies available for medical research—I am inclined to think that the key issue is whether one knowingly uses evil means and not whether one actually intends the evil means. But this is not the place for a full discussion of the issue this raises.)

Rational Action

If I am right, holism is wrong in its claim that side effects and foreseen consequences ought to be always as intended as means (usually) and ends (always) are. Why then does holism seem so plausible? The reason, I suggest, is that holism as an account of rational action represents one possible idealization of ordinary practice.

"Rational" is an evaluative term, so to talk about rational action is to talk about some sort of ideal case. An action that fails to be rational falls short of the ideal in some way or other. Different conceptions of rationality differ in which features of action they idealize and in the extent of the idealization made. My point is that holism represents quite an extreme idealization. I suggest that we also consider less extreme idealizations in which rational action involves the ideal following of the more ordinary procedures to which we mortals are restricted.

In a less extreme idealization an action might count as rational if it results from or is at least in accord with methods of decision that are rational for one to use. Such a principle would rule out holism, since it is not cost-effective for one to try to follow a holistic strategy and therefore not rational for one to do so.

When is a procedure rational in this sense? One necessary condition is that a rational procedure be in "rational equilibrium" so that the ideal following of the procedure would not lead one to modify it. A method of the sort I have outlined will normally be in rational equilibrium. Occasionally circumstances will make it salient that certain advantages can be gained by changing one's procedure in some way, and then until the change is made one's method of decision making will not be in rational equilibrium.

It might be that one could do better in ordinary life if one were to change one's procedure in certain ways, although one is now unaware of this. Perhaps this fact is even a logical consequence of things one is aware of but is the sort of thing only statisticians are familiar with. Then one's decision method may still be in rational equilibrium, despite its provable inefficiency, since use of that method may give one no reason to make the sort of mathematical or logical study required in order to discover what improvements might be made. In that case, I would count one's current procedure "rational." To express its disadvantages when compared with the other, better method, I prefer to use the term "provably inefficient." I suggest then that one's current procedure can be rational even if it is thus provably inefficient.

Do we need a term to designate the outcome that would be reached by the holistic method, ideally followed? No, if only because there is no determinate outcome to the holistic method, since that outcome depends on fixing subjective probabilities and utilities, and these are not determined in practice.

My conclusion, then, is that we are right to distinguish as we do between intended ends and means on the one hand and merely foreseen side effects and consequences on the other. In particular, the principle of Double Effect can be defended against attacks based on holism. It is even possible that the considerations I have mentioned might help to motivate a form of Double Effect or some similar principle, but I have not yet seen how that might be so. Whether these considerations positively support or motivate a principle like Double Effect must remain a matter for further investigations.

Practical and Theoretical Reasoning

What distinguishes practical reasoning from theoretical reasoning? It would seem that, if intending to do something does not involve believing one will do it, then we can accept our original answer that appeared at the beginning of chapter 1: practical reasoning revises intentions; theoretical reasoning revises beliefs, sometimes by connecting beliefs about what one intends to do with beliefs about what one will actually do. On the other hand, if intention does involve belief, matters are possibly more complicated, since the principles of practical reasoning must then restrict one to accepting only those intentions whose accompanying belief can also be accepted. So the revision of belief is sometimes "part of" practical reasoning.

To this it might be objected that there is no such restriction on practical reasoning and that at best there is only a restriction on the way we talk. In this view the point is merely that, if a practical conclusion is not accompanied by belief, we simply do not call it "intending," although we may say one has the relevant "intention."

Quite apart from this purely verbal issue, there are at least some restrictions on practical reasoning of this sort. Normally, one's decisions are and must be of a sort envisioned in the "simple case" of practical reasoning, and in that case one must believe one will do what one intends to do. Intending to do something must normally involve believing one will do it even if there are exceptions. Theoretical and practical reasoning are therefore intertwined.

Chapter 10
Review and Recapitulation

We have been concerned with the principles of reasoning, where reasoning is conceived as reasoned revision. Reasoning in this sense must not be confused with proof or argument, and the theory of reasoning must not be confused with logic. Psychological relations of immediate implication and immediate inconsistency are important in reasoning, but this is not to say that logical implication and logical inconsistency are of any special relevance.

Reasoning is subject to constraints of feasibility and practicality. So, the principles of reasoning are principles for revising all-or-nothing yes/no beliefs and plans; it is too complicated to try to operate generally with degrees of belief or probabilities. To be sure, there are degrees of belief: Belief is explicitly a matter of degree when one has an explicit belief about the probability of something; belief is more usually implicitly a matter of degree given one's all-or-nothing yes/no beliefs and the principles followed in revising such beliefs. But we could not always operate in terms of explicit probabilities. In particular, the use of probabilistic conditionalization as a method of updating one's degrees of belief is severely limited by a combinatorial explosion in resources needed.

Similarly, although in revising one's view it would be useful to have a record of one's reasons for various beliefs, this would involve too much record keeping. We could not in practice make use of a principle of negative undermining, which has one abandon any belief for which one does not have a current justification. Following that principle would lead one to abandon almost everything one believes. Instead, one must make do with a principle of positive undermining, which takes any current belief to be justified as long as there is no special reason to give it up.

Aspects of one's view can be accepted in different ways. Some aspects are fully accepted; some are accepted as provisional working hypotheses. Some are accepted for the moment, in the course of an argument; some are accepted as things to be remembered. Some are accepted merely personally, for oneself only; some are accepted in a more authoritative way as things that can be passed on to others. Different principles apply to these different types of acceptance. For example, reasons for accepting something as a working hypothesis are not sufficient for the sort of full acceptance which ends inquiry.

Principles for revising what one fully accepts promote conservatism and coherence. Conservatism is reflected in the principle that current beliefs are justified in the absence of any special challenge to them and in the principle of clutter avoidance, which limits newly inferred conclusions to those in which one has a reason to be interested. Coherence is reflected in one's disposition to avoid inconsistency and a tendency to promote explanatory and implicational connections among one's beliefs. (Perhaps the relevant implications are explanatory, so that all coherence is explanatory coherence.)

Practical reasoning is distinguished from theoretical reasoning by being in the first instance concerned with the revision of plans and intentions rather than beliefs. Like theoretical reasoning, practical reasoning is subject to principles of conservatism and coherence. But desires play a role in practical reasoning they do not play in theoretical reasoning, where ultimate desires must be distinguished from merely instrumental desires because of a difference in role such desires play in practical reasoning.

None of this pretends to be the last word on the subject. My aim has not been to settle issues but to raise issues. My aim has been to show that there is a subject here, change in view, a subject worthy of serious systematic study.

Appendix A
More on Logic and Reasoning

Natural Deduction

We can think some more about whether logic is specially relevant to reasoning by considering the following hypothesis:

Natural Deduction Hypothesis Certain basic patterns of logical implication and inconsistency are (psychologically) immediate.

For example, one might be disposed to take any two propositions P and Q immediately to imply their conjunction P & Q, and conversely one might be disposed to treat as immediate the logical implication from the conjunction P & Q to either of its conjuncts P or Q. Similarly, one might be disposed to take any proposition P to be immediately inconsistent with its denial *not P*. One might have these general dispositions even if, for sufficiently complicated or lengthy P and Q, one did not have the corresponding particular dispositions.

This by itself would not show logic is specially privileged, since various patterns of nonlogical implication and inconsistency might also be immediate in the relevant sense. For example, *X is part of Y* and *Y is part of Z* seem immediately to imply *X is part of Z* and seem to be immediately inconsistent with *X is not part of Z*. But these are not examples of logical implication and inconsistency, at least not in classical first-order predicate logic.

Three possible views might be taken about these last examples. First, we might conclude that not all immediate implications and inconsistencies are purely logical. Second, we might hold to the view that all immediate implications and inconsistencies are purely logical and claim that logic includes part-whole logic. Third, we might hold the view that all immediate implications and inconsistencies are purely logical but deny that logic includes part-whole logic and take the implication from *X is part of Y* and *Y is part of Z* to *X is part of Z* to be mediated by the nonlogical principles that, if one thing is part of another and the second is part of a third, then the first is part of the third.

How can we decide among these possibilities? Before we try to answer that question, let us consider another, related issue.

Defining Logical Constants

It might be suggested that, whether or not basic logical implications and inconsistencies are the only psychologically immediate implications and inconsistencies, logic is distinctive in being entirely derivable from psychologically immediate implications and inconsistencies. The idea is that any logical implication or inconsistency is either immediate or provable from immediate implications and/or inconsistencies in a series of immediate steps; furthermore, this distinguishes logic from other subjects. In this view logic is a distinctive subject in being entirely either obvious or potentially obvious.

But what distinguishes one subject from another? The suggestion fails if there are nonlogical immediate implications and if any arbitrary body of implications constitutes a subject. Then the "subject" consisting of logic plus any given set of nonlogical immediate implications is entirely either obvious or potentially obvious. So, for example, logic plus the obvious principles of chemistry would count as logic, by this criterion.

It is natural to distinguish subjects by their central concepts. But we can't suppose that *all* implications involving logical concepts are obvious or potentially obvious, since there are many nonlogical implications involving these notions. The principle, "if something burns with a yellow flame, it contains sodium," is not obvious, although it uses the logical notion "if."

The suggestion has to be that certain *crucial* implications (and inconsistencies) involving these notions are immediate or potentially immediate. In particular, let us now consider the more or less familiar suggestion that logical concepts are distinctive in that their *content* can be characterized entirely in terms of their function in reasoning, more specifically in terms of immediate implication and inconsistency.

This presupposes conceptual role semantics (Harman 1982a) or functionalism (Fodor 1983) as a theory of the content of psychological attitudes. In this view the meanings of words are derivative from the concepts these words are used to express, and the contents of the associated concepts are (at least partly) determined by the way those concepts are used in thought.

In this view there are at least three basic types of possible use of a concept: (1) the perceptual categorization of what one perceives, (2) the use of concepts in getting oneself to act in one way or another, and (3) the use of concepts in reasoning to get from some thoughts to others

(Sellars 1963). It might be held that the contents of key logical concepts can be specified entirely in terms of their third, intermediate use in reasoning. In particular, the suggestion is that logical notions can be specified entirely in terms of their role in thought as reflected in immediate implication and immediate inconsistency.

There is a superficial resemblance between this suggestion and various other attempts that have been made to explain logical notions entirely in terms of principles of "natural deduction" or of the "sequent calculus" (Gentzen 1935; Popper 1947; Kneale 1956; Shoesmith and Smiley 1978; Hacking 1979). But the present suggestion is not quite the same as any of those in these other approaches, which do not appeal to any notion of *immediate* implication or inconsistency. The hope is that the appeal to immediacy will yield some benefits not obtainable from the other approaches.

Let us consider how the present suggestion might be carried out. For conjunction, we might try something like this:

Definition of Logical Conjunction   C expresses logical conjunction if and only if C serves to combine two thoughts, P and Q, to form a third thought, C(P,Q), such that P and Q taken together immediately imply and are separately immediate implications of C(P,Q).

Logical disjunction might be defined similarly:

Definition of Logical Disjunction   D expresses logical disjunction if and only if D serves to combine two thoughts, P and Q, to form a third thought, D(P,Q), such that (1) D(P,Q) is immediately implied by each of P and Q taken individually, (2) D(P,Q) plus any set of propositions immediately inconsistent with P immediately imply Q, and (3) D(P,Q) plus any set of propositions immediately inconsistent with Q immediately imply P.

What about (classical) logical negation? This concept applies to a proposition P to give its denial, N(P). One feature of N is that N(P) is immediately inconsistent with P, but that is also true of any other contrary of P as well. What distinguishes N(P) from other contraries of P is that N(P) is the most inclusive contrary of P; it is implied by any other contrary of P, that is, by anything else excluded by P. (This is not true of intuitionistic negation, which allows that *not not P* may fail to imply P.) So, we might try the following definition:

Definition of (Classical) Logical Negation   N expresses logical negation if and only if N applies to a thought, P, to form a second thought, N(P), such that N(P) is immediately inconsistent with P

and is immediately implied by any set of propositions that is immediately inconsistent with P; furthermore, any set of propositions
immediately inconsistent with $N(P)$ immediately imply P.

Given this definition we can account for the following:

> *Reductio Ad Absurdum*   If A is immediately inconsistent, any set
> of propositions F together with "F, P *imply A*" immediately imply
> *not P*.

For, if A is immediately inconsistent, so are F, P, and "F, P *imply A*."
Then, by the definition of negation, it follows that F, "F, P *imply A*"
imply *not P*.

Logical quantification ("everything" and "something") is more complicated. The relevant principles would be principles of instantiation
and generalization. In order to state such principles, we have to say
what it is for a proposition to be an instance of a quantified proposition,
when an instance is immediately implied by a quantified proposition
of which it is an instance, and when a quantified proposition is immediately implied by an instance of it. Given that the notion of an
instance has been explained, we can give a partial account of the relevant
immediate implications by noting that a universal quantification immediately implies any of its instances, and an existential quantification
is immediately implied by any of its instances.

We also have to say something about universal instantiation and
existential generalization. We might end up with a definition roughly
similar to the following for universal quantification:

> *Definition of Universal Quantification*   A variable binding operator
> "( )" represents universal quantification if and only if (1) $(x)P(x)$
> immediately implies any instance $P(a)$ and (2) "*the propositions F
> imply any P(a) no matter what a is taken to refer to*" immediately
> implies "*the propositions F imply (x)Px.*"

A similar definition of existential quantification might be given.

It might be objected that these definitions do not distinguish logical
concepts from other concepts that are equivalent to them but not synonymous with them. For example, it might be suggested that the concept
expressed by "... or ... or $1 = 2$" serves to combine two thoughts,
P and Q, to form a third thought, "P or Q or $1 = 2$" in a way that
satisfies the Definition of Logical Disjunction, although this more complex concept is not synonymous with logical disjunction. The suggestion
is that P immediately implies "P or Q or $1 = 2$" (and so does Q);
furthermore, if A is immediately inconsistent with P, then A and "P
or Q or $1 = 2$ immediately imply Q (and similarly with P and Q reversed).

A possible reply is to deny the second part of this suggestion, holding that the implication from "P or Q or 1 = 2" and A to Q is not immediate but involves at least two steps, one dropping P from the disjunction, the other dropping 1 = 2. Similar replies might be made to other proposed counterexamples of this sort. If such replies are successful, this sort of objection fails.

It is hard to say whether this reply succeeds, since it is not clear when implications are immediate. Since immediate implication is a psychological matter having to do with a person's cognitive dispositions, such a reply seems to involve a substantive hypothesis about what can and cannot be immediate for a person, no matter how experienced or practiced the person may be. I discuss this sort of hypothesis subsequently. For now, let us keep an open mind on the issue.

If the reply fails and the objection succeeds, things get complicated. It becomes necessary to modify the definitions of the logical constants. One thing wrong with the more complex concept is that, although it may satisfy the definition as stated, it also has aspects of content that are not mentioned in that definition. This suggests adding that the characterization given must completely characterize the content of D. For example:

> *Definition of Logical Disjunction*   D expresses logical disjunction if and only if D serves to combine two thoughts, P and Q, to form a third thought, D(P,Q), where the content of D can be entirely characterized by saying (1) D(P,Q) is immediately implied by each of P and Q taken individually, (2) D(P,Q) plus any set of propositions immediately inconsistent with P immediately imply Q, and (3) D(P,Q) plus any set of propositions immediately inconsistent with Q immediately imply P.

Similar modifications would have to be made in the other definitions. These definitions would then put considerable weight on the idea that the content of a logical concept can be entirely characterized by citing certain principles. The content of the concept is supposed to be minimal in the sense that the concept has no more content beyond what follows from the role the concept has by virtue of satisfying the cited principles. That is what is supposed to rule out the connective, ". . . or . . . or 1 = 2," as an instance of logical disjunction.

But it is obscure just what it could mean to say that the content of a concept is "entirely characterized in terms of" certain principles. In what way would the content have to be minimal? Because of this obscurity, it is not clear what to say about the suggestion that, if we can appeal to the notion that certain rules entirely characterize a concept, we do not need to include an appeal to the rule that a conjunction is implied by its conjuncts taken together as long as we can appeal to the rule that a conjunction implies either of its conjuncts. The suggestion is, in other words, that we might make do with the following definition:

> *Simpler Definition of Logical Conjunction*   C expresses logical conjunction if and only if C serves to combine two thoughts, P and Q, to form a third thought, C(P,Q), where the content of C can be entirely characterized by saying that P and Q are separately immediately implied by C(P,Q).

In this view, to say that the content of C can be entirely characterized by citing this one principle is to say that C is a minimal concept satisfying the principle, that is, that C(P,Q) is entailed by any other K(P,Q), where K is a concept that satisfies this principle and perhaps others as well. It would seem that any such minimal concept C must have the property that P and Q jointly imply C(P,Q), for the content of C(P,Q) includes at least that of P and of Q, since these are both implied by C(P,Q). Furthermore, it should include no more than this, since C is the minimal concept satisfying that condition. But, if C was not implied by P and Q taken together, it would seem that C(P,Q) must include more than that. So C(P,Q) would seem to be implied by P and Q taken together.

We could not in the same way defend defining conjunction solely in terms of the rule that P and Q taken together imply C(P,Q). The content of C(P,Q) could be as minimal as a tautology and still satisfy that rule, since a tautology is implied by anything. Conjunction is therefore not the minimal notion satisfying that condition. But one might defend that latter definition in an analogous way, since a conjunction is a *maximal* thought that follows from its conjuncts taken together, at least in the sense that the conjunction implies any other thought that follows from those conjuncts. It might be suggested that a concept is entirely characterized by certain principles only if it is a logically maximal concept involved in constructions that the principles say are implied by certain things and/or if it is a logically minimal concept involved in constructions that the principles say imply certain things. (This rule cannot apply if a logically maximal concept that is involved in constructions that the principles say are implied by certain things is not the same as a logically minimal concept involved in constructions that the principles say imply certain things.)

It might be objected that these arguments for simplifying the Definition of Conjunction are incomplete. Even if it can be shown that any concept C satisfying the Simpler Definition of Logical Conjunction is such that P and Q jointly imply C(P,Q), that does not show that this last implication is *immediate*, which seems necessary if C is to be a conjunction.

This still leaves open the question of whether we can in this way use such simpler definitions to specify concepts that are equivalent to conjunction even if they are not strictly synonymous with conjunction (as previously defined). This is unclear because it is unclear whether either or both of the (partial) interpretations of "entirely characterized" appealed to is acceptable, given the obscurity of "entirely characterized."

Is Logic Specially Relevant to Reasoning?

It is at the very least unclear whether it is possible to specify basic logical concepts in terms of immediate implication and inconsistency, treated as basic notions of the theory of reasoning. If that is possible, there would be at least one important connection between logic and reasoning. But, even if this connection existed, that would not mean logic tells us something about reasoning. It would mean only that basic logical constants can be defined partly in terms of basic concepts of the theory of reasoning. In particular, notice that these definitions say only what it is for a concept to be the concept of negation or whatever. The definitions do not entail that ordinary people actually make use of such logical notions. (And it is controversial whether ordinary people make use of the concept of classical logical negation, for example.) Nor would the definitions entail that logic is especially relevant to reasoning even if people do or did make use of logical notions.

We have already observed that some immediate implications do not seem to be logical implications. *X is part of Y* and *Y is part of Z* seem immediately to imply *X is part of Z*. *Today is Thursday* seems immediately to imply *Tomorrow is Friday*. These do not seem to be logical implications. They are certainly not part of classical logic.

Now, consider the following hypothesis:

> *Only Logic Is Immediate*   The only really immediate implications are logical. Other seemingly immediate implications actually involve recognition of several intermediate steps.

Given this hypothesis, one might suggest either that the first implication (about parts) depends on an unstated premise or that the part-whole relation is a logical relation. Faced with the implication from *Today is Thursday* to *Tomorrow is Friday*, one might suggest that this implication is not really immediate, but involves something like the following steps:

1. Today is Thursday. (Assumption)
2. Tomorrow is the day after today. (Assumption)
3. Friday is the day after Thursday. (Assumption)

4. The day after today is the day after today. (Assumption)
5. The day after today is the day after Thursday. (From steps 1 and 4)
6. Tomorrow is the day after Thursday. (From steps 2 and 5)
7. Tomorrow is Friday. (From steps 3 and 6)

Alternatively, one might take the implication from *Today is Thursday* to *Tomorrow is Friday* to be an immediate implication and suppose that it is, after all, a logical implication, where the relevant logic is some sort of temporal logic—a tense logic plus a days of the week logic.

In order to test such suggestions, we need an independent criterion of immediacy and an independent criterion of logic. Otherwise we could arbitrarily either retain classical logic and treat all apparently immediate implications as mediated by various nonlogical principles, as in steps 1–7, or abandon classical logic and count all apparently immediate implications as logical implications or adopt any one of various intermediate positions. In the absence of criteria of immediacy and of logic, these ideas are not clearly competing, nor do they clearly compete with the (seemingly more natural) idea that only some immediate implications are logical.

Principles of Truth

Sometimes there are considerations that make one or another option implausible. Consider that everyone can easily recognize any implication of the following form:

Knowledge Schema   P knows that S implies *S*.

If one wants to retain the idea that Only Logic Is Immediate, one has two options. First, one might hold these are instances of a logical principle in a *logic* of knowledge in which "know" is a logical constant. Second, one might opt for a *theory* of knowledge, taking these implications to be mediated by the general principle that whatever one knows is true. However, this second option simply pushes the problem back to truth, since it involves an appeal to an appropriate instance of the following schema:

Truth Schema   It is true that S implies *S*.

The same two options apply in this case. First, one might hold these are instances of a logical principle in the *logic* of truth, in which "true" is a logical constant. Second, one might suppose these implications are mediated by principles in a *theory* of truth.

What sort of theory might this be? It might be suggested that the theory has infinitely many principles, one for each instance of the Truth Schema. Each such principle might be a statement of the form, "If it is true that *S, S.*" But this cannot be anyone's *explicit* view of the matter, since one cannot have infinitely many explicit representations in one's mind. Our recognition of the implications that are instances of the Truth Schema cannot be mediated by the principles of such an infinite theory. (Nor can our recognition of the implications that are instances of the Knowledge Schema be mediated by principles of the corresponding infinite theory of knowledge.)

If our recognition of the various implications that are instances of the Truth Schema is mediated by a theory of truth, the relevant theory must consist in a finite number of principles that imply all these instances. There seem to be two ways in which this could be so.

First, the theory might consist in a single principle using *second-order* quantification:

Second-Order Truth Principle   (S) (if it is true that S, then S).

It is not easy to express this in English (Stebbins 1980). One might try to put the principle like this: "If something is true, then it." But that doesn't make sense. One needs to add "then it is true," which changes the principle into a trivial one. Or one might instead say, "then it is so," but that is only verbally different; the word "so" functions here as a variant of "true."

Of course, the fact that we do not have any easy way to express this principle in ordinary English does not mean the principle itself is unintelligible. Indeed, it is possible to make sense of such second-order quantification (e.g., Jeffrey 1981). However, it seems unlikely that anyone who has not studied formal logic accepts such a principle. So it does not seem plausible to suppose that the implications of the Truth Schema are mediated by a Second-Order Truth Principle for ordinary people.

We have been considering whether these implications might be mediated by principles in a finite theory of truth and have suggested that one way in which this might be thought to happen cannot be the right story. Similar remarks hold for a "prosentential" theory of truth, which takes *it is true that S* to be simply a variant of *S* (Grover et al. 1975). In this prosentential view, the Truth Schema reduces to the trivial point that *S* implies *S*. Such a prosentential theory has to appeal to second-order quantification to handle remarks such as "What Bob said is true." So it too cannot represent ordinary thinking about truth.

A different possibility is that the implications of the Truth Schema are mediated by a number of more ordinary first-order principles. Such principles might include the following:

1. If a proposition consisting of a predicate and a name is true, the predicate applies to the thing named by the name.
2. *Dobbin* names Dobbin.
3. The predicate *is a horse* applies to all and only horses.
4. A conjunction is true if and only if its conjuncts are true.

It may be that, following Taksi (1956), such a first-order theory can be developed. However, in any such theory, the number of intermediate steps between *It is true that S* and S would have to increase in proportion to the complexity of "S". So, if a person's recognition of such implications were mediated by these intermediate steps, we would expect this recognition to be more difficult and to take more time, in proportion to the complexity of S. But his expectation is simply false. All that is needed to recognize the implication in any instance of the Truth Schema is to recognize that it is the same S both times. It is psychologically implausible that one's recognition of such implications is mediated by the principles in a finite first-order theory of truth.

This strongly suggests that instances of the Truth Schema are immediate implications, which means the hypothesis that Only Logic Is Immediate can be accepted only by taking these instances to be instances of logical principles, in which case logic must include a logic of truth in which "true" is a logical constant.

The suggestion that "true" is a logical constant fits in well with the suggestion that logical constants are notions whose content is completely captured by relations of immediate implication and immediate inconsistency. It is plausible that the content of the predicate "true," as we ordinarily understand it, can be entirely characterized by citing the Biconditional Truth Schema if we go on to note that (because of the liar paradox) instances of the schema are acceptable only "other things being equal" as "default assumptions" that are to be abandoned if they lead to trouble. And perhaps instances of the Conditional Truth Schema are always acceptable, since these by themselves do not lead to trouble.

The supposition that "true" is a logical constant conflicts with certain other ways of characterizing logic. For instance, I have suggested elsewhere that logical constants in a natural language are grammatically distinctive in always being members of small, closed logical classes of terms (Harman 1982b). "True" is not such a term, since there are many adjectives and verbs that are relevantly similar to it in taking a "that" clause complement—"surprising," "probable," "fortunate," "believe," "hope," "fear," etc. On the other hand terms for identity and set membership, which are often taken to be logical constants, also fail to count as logical terms by this grammatical criterion. So we might just reject any such grammatical criterion of logic (that is, we might observe that logic defined in that way is less closely tied to reasoning than is logic defined in terms of immediate implication and inconsistency). If we do count the relevant instances of the Biconditional Truth Schema as logical implications, it would seem impossible to refute the hypothesis that Only Logic Is Immediate, for, whenever there seems to be a general pattern of immediate implication that is not a purely logical pattern, one can always say the implication is mediated by the nonlogical principle that, whenever propositions of this or that sort are true, the corresponding proposition of such and such a sort is also true. It is not clear how such a claim could be refuted.

Of course, this is not to say the claim is therefore proved! One can still consistently suppose there are nonlogical immediate implications, but it is unclear how there could be any fact of the matter as to which supposition is really correct.

Appendix B
"Ought" and Reasons

In this book I use the phrase "practical reasoning" to refer to the reasoned revision of intentions, but others use this phrase differently. In chapter 1 I noted the view that practical reasoning consists in the construction of an argument of a special practical sort, a practical syllogism, or an argument in the logic of imperatives. I suggested that this idea rests on confusing reasoning in the sense of argument construction with reasoning in the sense of making a reasoned revision in one's view.

In chapter 8 I mentioned that some writers use the term "practical reasoning" to refer to reasoning that might culminate in a belief about what one ought to do or what one has reasons to do. For example, Davidson (1978) argues that the upshot of practical reasoning is an "all-out" evaluative judgment that a certain act is the best thing to do. Williams (1980) takes practical reasoning to be a process of arriving at an "all-in" judgment about what one has reasons to do—what one has reasons to do, all things considered. Nagel (1970) takes practical reasoning to be concerned with establishing that one has certain (prima facie) reasons to do things (reasons that may be overridden by other reasons). And various writers suppose that practical reasoning leads to a conclusion about what one *ought* to do.

In the terminology I have adopted, all such reasoning is *theoretical* reasoning, since it revises *beliefs* about what one has reasons to do or about what one ought to do. The matter is a delicate one: these beliefs are (I think) themselves beliefs *about* practical reasoning. They are not directly practical conclusions but are theoretical conclusions about practical conclusions.

Reasons

To say that a consideration C is a reason to do D is, I suggest, to say that C is a consideration that has or ought to have some influence on reasoning, leading to a decision to do D unless this is overruled by other considerations. The consideration *C* might be an end or a belief one has, or it might be some line of thought which one finds or would find attractive or persuasive on reflection, for example, an argument of some sort.

Sometimes we cite as a reason a consideration that the agent is unaware of, either because the agent has not thought of something or because the agent lacks information. But I think the basic case is one in which the consideration cited is indeed one the agent is aware of and properly appreciates. Other cases can be understood in relation to that case, citing a consideration that would influence the agent if he or she were aware of it and made no mistakes in reasoning.

Sometimes we distinguish saying that a given person *S* "has a reason" to do *A* from saying that "there is a reason" for *S* to do *A*. The distinction is partly due to an ambiguity in the latter statement between the interpretation, "there is a reason for it to happen that *S* does *A*" (which might be either a reason to believe *S* will do *A* or a reason to be in favor of *S*'s doing *A*), where the reason is not taken to be a reason of *S*'s, and the different interpretation, "there is a reason for *S* (or of *S*'s) for *S* to do *A*." This second interpretation is similar in meaning to "*S* has a reason to do *A*," except that "*S* has a reason to do *A*" suggests that the reason is either known to *S* or is almost within *S*'s grasp. "There is a reason for *S* to do *A*," meaning a reason *for S*, seems to allow for a bit more distance between the envisioned reason and *S*. But this difference in meaning is vague.

An all-in or all-out or all-things-considered judgment that the weight of reasons favors doing *D* is, I suggest, a judgment that reasoning does or should lead one to form the intention of doing *D* (or should lead one simply to do *D*, for example, if doing *D* is *believing something*). It is a judgment about the ideal outcome of reasoning.

"Ought" and Other Modals

In order to understand judgments using *"ought"* and *"should,"* it is useful to note that these terms are part of a family of modal terms including *"may," "might," "can," "could," "must," "has to," "is necessary,"* and *"is possible."* Such terms can be used to express different kinds of modality and different strengths of a given kind of modality (Wertheimer 1972).

As far as strength goes, *"ought"* and *"should"* are intermediate in strength between the stronger terms *"must," "have to,"* and *"is necessary,"* and the weaker terms *"may," "might," "can,"* and *"could."* So, for example, it makes sense to say Jane *may* spend the money on herself, although she *ought* to give it to charity. She *ought* to give it to charity but she doesn't *have to*.

It is traditional to distinguish at least the following kinds of modality (Lacey 1976). (1) *Epistemic modality* is concerned with what is certain, probable, likely to be false, and so on. In cooking a six-pound chicken, after 30 minutes Brian judges that it *can't* be done yet. After 90 minutes, he thinks that it *might* be done. After 2 hours he concludes that it *ought* to be done by now. If it isn't and he cooks it for another half hour, he thinks now it *has* to be done. All these are judgments of epistemic modality. (2) *Alethic modality* is concerned with what can or could happen in the world, given the laws of metaphysics or the laws of nature, whether or not anyone realizes this and whether or not it would be a good thing for that to happen. We say that nothing *can* travel faster than the speed of light, that perpetual motion is *impossible*, and that an unsupported heavy body *must* fall to the ground. These are judgments of alethic modality. There do not seem to be judgments of alethic modality using *ought*, unless we count judgments such as that a tree ought to have strong roots, a heart ought to beat regularly, and so on. (3) *Deontic modality* is concerned with the normative or evaluative assessment of situations or people. We may judge that Jane *ought* morally to give the money to charity, although morally she does not *have to*, since she *could* spend it on herself, but she *can't* use it to try to bribe the judge in the poodle contest.

The traditional classification of modality provides only a rough guide. For one thing, the category of deontic modality covers several distinct notions.

"Ought to Do" and "Ought to Be"

Consider the following example from Humberstone (1971). Children are working in a sweatshop. An observer remarks, "Children ought not to work under such conditions," intending to say something about the situation the children find themselves in. This is a remark about what ought not to be the case, not a remark about what the children ought to do about it. The speaker means that the situation is wrong, not that the children are wrong to participate as they do. The speaker does not mean it is wrong of them to work under such conditions. The speaker means that there are reasons for this not to happen, not that the children have reasons to refrain from participating.

Now consider a different example in which some children are teasing a boy. An observer remarks, "The children ought not to torment little Eddie so." This is not just a remark about what ought not to be the case, it is also a remark about what the children ought to do about it.

The speaker implies that the children are wrong to act as they do, that it is wrong *of* them to torment little Eddie, maybe that there is something wrong *with* them if they torture Eddie. Perhaps it implies that they have sufficient reason not to torment little Eddie.

The first sort of judgment is a judgment about what *ought to be*, whereas the second sort of judgment is a judgment about what someone *ought to do* (Castaneda 1972).

The distinction is important, since, for example, certain moral theories, such as utilitarianism, gain apparent plausibility through conflating *ought-to-be* judgments with *ought-to-do* judgments (Harman 1983). Utilitarianism conflates saying "What one ought to do is bring about X" with "What ought to be the case is that one bring about X."

The distinction applies to stronger and weaker judgments, too. An observer might say, "Children must not work under such conditions," or, contrastingly, "It is OK for children to work under such conditions." These are stronger and weaker judgments of a situation in which children work under these conditions, corresponding to the *"ought to be."* On the other hand an observer might say, "They must not torment little Eddie," or, contrastingly, "They are not wrong to torment him," making stronger and weaker judgments of the children and not just of the situation.

The "Ought" of Reasons

Sometimes an *"ought"* judgment is used to indicate that someone has reasons to do something. Fred might say to Mabel, "You *ought* to take the turnpike; it is the fastest way to get where you want to go, even though it is somewhat longer than taking Route 9. You *could* take Route 30; of course, that is not nearly as fast, but there is much less traffic. But you *cannot* take Route 1, since you won't arrive on time if you do that. That would be the *wrong* thing to do."

Just as we can distinguish mentioning a consideration that is *a* reason, not necessarily the only relevant one, from saying what someone has reason to do *"all things considered"* (Davidson's all-out judgment, or Williams' all-in judgment), we can distinguish saying what someone *ought* "prima facie" to do from what he or she *ought* to do "all things considered." Fred can say, "Given only that you want to get there in a hurry, you ought to take Route 95. Given only that you want to avoid traffic, you ought to take Route 30. Taking everything into account, you ought to take Route 9, since it is almost as fast as Route 95 and there is less traffic."

Moral, Legal, and Other "Ought"'s

Often, to say someone *ought morally* to do something is to imply that he or she has moral reasons to do it; to say someone *ought legally* to do something is to imply he or she has legal reasons to do it, and so on. Such judgments might be either prima facie judgments or all-things-considered judgments.

But it is not true that "S ought morally to do A" means that S's doing A is what the moral considerations support, nor that "S's ought legally to do A" means that S's doing A is what the legal considerations support, and so on. We can use *"ought morally," "ought legally,"* and so on to make a moral, legal, or whatever judgment that takes all considerations into account. Morality allows for the balancing of all considerations, moral and other, for example, self-interested considerations, in arriving at a judgment of what one ought to do all things considered. For example, one might decide that, from the moral point of view, the moral considerations outweigh the more petty self-interested considerations in a particular case and conclude that one ought morally to do something all things considered. Or one might decide that, from the moral point of view, certain, more serious self-interested considerations outweigh a relatively trivial promise, so that, morally, one may break one's promise. Similarly, the law allows that certain legal requirements can be overridden, for example, by sufficiently strong considerations of self-interest so that legally one is excused from acting in a way in which one would otherwise be required to act. In an emergency it may not be legally wrong to park in a "No Parking" area.

It is sometimes suggested that *"ought morally"* simply coincides with *"ought, all things considered."* But that is not true. Henry has a moral reason to take his next door neighbor's eight-year-old daughter, Lucy, to the big game this afternoon, since he promised her he would do so and she has been looking forward to it. But Henry also has a strong self-interested reason not to take Lucy to the game and to spend the afternoon with his broker instead. If enough money is involved, we might well think that all things considered Henry ought to go to his broker, even though this means disappointing Lucy. But we would not express this conclusion by saying that Henry *ought morally* to go to his broker. So, *"ought, all things considered"* is not synonymous with *"ought morally."* (Here we might say, "All things considered Henry *may* morally go to his broker.")

A more plausible and somewhat weaker suggestion is that it can never be true that all things considered one ought morally to do one thing and all things considered one ought (without the *morally*) not to do that but to do something else. (Or perhaps what is plausible is that this can never be true unless *"ought"* is being used, in what Hare (1952) calls the inverted commas sense, to mean *"what some group of people think or say one ought to do."*)

This suggests there is not a special *moral* sense of *"ought."* Rather, when the *"ought"* of reasons is in question and what one ought to do all things considered is a course of action for which one's moral reasons are controlling, then we say one *ought morally* to do it. If the moral considerations in favor of an act are sufficiently compelling, we say one *morally has to* do it. We say one *morally may* do something if it isn't true that one *morally has to do it* or *ought morally to do it.*

To what extent do similar conclusions apply to *"ought legally," "ought from the point of view of etiquette,"* etc.? The law says no parking is allowed in a certain area, so one has a legal reason not to park there. However, one also has a self-interested reason to park there, because it is a convenient spot. Perhaps, all things considered, one ought to park there. Could this be expressed as "Legally, one shouldn't park there, but all things considered one should park there anyway"? This seems acceptable language to me.

It might be suggested that this is an inverted commas use: "According to the law, one shouldn't park there." But then the question is whether there is anything other than an inverted commas use for legal judgments. Why not suppose that *"legally"* always means *"according to law"*?

For that matter, why not always suppose that *"morally"* always means *"according to morality"*? To this last question there are two related answers. First, when we say that someone ought morally to do something, we usually presuppose acceptance of some morality and speak from within that perspective so as to express a favorable attitude toward the agent's acting in that way. In other words someone who accepts a morality can make judgments from within that morality which are not just inverted commas judgments. Second, a judgment about what is so, according to a morality, is a judgment about the way things look to someone who accepts that morality. It is not just a judgment about what follows deductively from certain moral principles, given the facts, since there is no way to capture the weighing of considerations against each other in a deductive calculus. Such a judgment can be understood only in terms of the reactions of someone who accepts that morality. In saying that, according to a given morality, all things considered *S* ought to do *A*, we seem to mean roughly this: If *S*, accepting the relevant morality, were to be aware of all the relevant considerations and reasoned correctly, then *S* would decide to do *A*.

The same is true of law. A judgment that *S* ought to do *A*, according to the law, is not the judgment that this conclusion follows deductively from certain legal principles together with the facts of the case. This is true for the same reason as for moral judgments, namely, that there is no way to capture the balancing of considerations against each other in a deductive calculus. Here too, such judgments are judgments about decisions that would be made by someone who accepts law as binding and who reasons without error in the light of all the relevant facts. (Dworkin (1977) offers a model of this that appeals to an idealized judge. But that is a lawyer's prejudice. It is more accurate to appeal here, as in the moral case to an idealized agent.)

Functional Evaluation

Sometimes *"ought"* or *"should"* is used to express an evaluation of something in terms of some associated function, need, role, normal case or ideal. A heart *ought* to pump at a regular rate; if it does not, there is something *wrong* with it. A tree *should* have strong roots; if it does, we say it has *good* roots. A paring knife *ought* to cut well. A teacher *ought* to help students acquire an interest in learning and an ability to learn. "Ideally, a plain yogurt *should* have some astringency as well as a sweet/sour character. . . " (*Consumer Reports*, August 1983, p. 386). There is *something wrong* with Tess that leads her to torment little Eddie like that.

A judgment of this sort made about a particular agent, as in the last example, need not imply that the agent has reasons to act in a certain way. We can feel there is something wrong *with* Tess without feeling that it is wrong *of* her that she acts in that way. (Perhaps Tess is afflicted with a compulsion of some sort.) However, a judgment of this sort is not just an evaluation of a situation, like the judgment, "It is wrong that children work under such conditions." It is an evaluation of an agent.

So, sometimes a moral judgment about a particular agent does not imply the agent has reasons to act in a certain way. It does not have that implication if it is an evaluation of the agent with respect to an ideal in this way. The difference is connected with whether it is appropriate to suppose it is *wrong of* the agent to fail to act as he or she *ought*, as opposed to supposing merely that there is somethings *wrong with* the agent if he or she fails to act as he or she ought to act.

Different Senses of "Ought"?

I have distinguished the following modalities:

1. Alethic: "An unsupported stone must fall to the ground."
2. Epistemic: "The train ought to be here soon."

3. Evaluative of a situation: "There can't be another war!"
4. Specifying reasons: "A thief ought to wear gloves." (Possible qualifications here with *"morally,"* *"legally,"* etc.)
5. Functional, etc. evaluation of something or someone in a situation: "That knife should be sharper."

There are further cases. For example, *"can"* is used in talking about a person's or thing's abilities, as when we say that Susan can swim.

Does all this really imply that there are various meanings or senses of modal terms such as *"must," "ought,"* and *"can"*? I am inclined to say yes, although it is sometimes not easy to tell which of these senses is being employed on a particular occasion. The remark, "The train ought to be here in a few minutes," may represent an epistemic claim, "We have every reason to think the train will be here in a few minutes," or an evaluative claim, "It is desirable for trains to be on schedule." A speaker may not have definitely decided between these intended interpretations. The same vagueness may affect judgments about what is *expected*, as in "Students were expected to purchase the textbook." Similarly, when we say Tom should not torment little Eddie so, we may not be clear in our own minds whether we mean to imply that Tom has reasons not to torment little Eddie; we may not have decided between the stronger thought that it is wrong *of* Tom to torment Eddie in that way and the weaker thought that something is wrong *with* Tom. There is a sensitive discussion of the general phenomenon of such multiple aspects (or "vectors") of meaning in Ziff (1972).

"Ought" and Reasons: No Regress

If we say that a *reason* is a consideration that *ought* to influence reasoning and if we also explain *"ought"* judgments as judgments about reasons, does this lead to a vicious, infinite regress? More precisely, consider the following four propositions:

1. *C* is a reason *S* has to do *A*.
2. *C* is a consideration that ought to influence *S*'s reasoning in the direction of a decision to do *A*.

3. *S* ought to be influenced by *C* in the direction of a decision to do *A*.
4. *S* has a reason to be influenced by *C* in the direction of a decision to do *A*.

It may seem that I have explained each of these propositions in terms of the one that follows, in which case the reason statement 1 would ultimately be explained in terms of the more complicated reason statement 4, so there would be a vicious infinite regress.

The resolution of this apparent difficulty is to observe that *"ought"* in 2 is a functional *"ought."* Statement 2 means C is a consideration that would ideally influence S's reasoning in the relevant way; that is, it would do so if nothing went wrong. Statement 3 follows from 2 if *"ought"* is understood in the same way as in 3, as a functional *"ought."* But then 3, so interpreted cannot be explained as 4. So the apparent difficulty rests on an equivocation in the meaning of *"ought."*

Summary

"Ought (to)" is a member of a class of modal verbs used to express various modalities. Other verbs in this class include *"must,"* *"has (to),"* *"should,"* *"may,"* *"might,"* *"can,"* and *"could."* These verbs vary in strength. They are used to express epistemic, alethic, and deontic modalities. Sometimes they are used to assess a situation or state of affairs; sometimes they are used to relate someone to a possible action.

"Ought" is sometimes used to assess a person's reasons for doing something. If the controlling reasons are moral, we say that someone ought morally to do something. We can also speak of what a person ought legally or ought according to etiquette to do, but this need not express what a person ought to do all things considered.

Finally, *"ought"* and related terms are sometimes used to make functional evaluations.

Bibliography

Achinstein, Peter (1983). *The Nature of Explanation* (New York: Oxford University Press).

Anderson, J. R., and Bower, G. H. (1973). *Human Associative Memory* (Washington, D. C.: Winston).

Anscombe, G. E. M. (1957). *Intention* (Oxford: Basil Blackwell).

Austin, J. L. (1946). "Other minds," *Proceedings of the Aristotelian Society*, supp. vol. 20: 148–187.

Beardsley, Monroe (1978). "Intending," in *Values and Morals*, Alvin I. Goldman and Jaegwon Kim, eds. (Dordrecht, Holland: Reidel), 163–184.

Bennett, Jonathan (1976). *Linguistic Behaviour* (Cambridge: Cambridge University Press).

Black, Max (1958). "Self-supporting inductive arguments," *Journal of Philosophy* 55:718–725.

Brandt, Richard (1979). *A Theory of the Good and the Right* (Oxford: Oxford University Press).

Bratman, Michael (to appear). "Two faces of intention," *Philosophical Review*.

Bromberger, Sylvain (1966). "Why-questions," in *Mind and Cosmos*, R. G. Colodny, ed. (Pittsburgh, Penn.: University of Pittsburgh Press), 86–108.

Castaneda, Hector-Neri (1972). "On the semantics of the ought to do," in *Semantics of Natural Language*, D. Davidson and G. Harman (Dordrecht, Holland: Reidel), 675–694.

Chisholm, Roderick (1966). "Freedom and action," in *Freedom and Determinism*, Keith Lehrer, ed. (New York: Random House), 11–44.

Davidson, Donald (1963). "Actions, reasons, and causes," *Journal of Philosophy* 60, 685–700.

Davidson, Donald (1973). "Freedom to act," in *Essays on Freedom of Action*, T. Honderich, ed. (London: Routledge and Kegan Paul), 137–156.

Davidson, Donald (1978). "Intending," in *Philosophy of History and Action*, Yirmiaku Yovel, ed. (Dordrecht, Holland: Reidel).

Dennett, Daniel C. (1978). *Brainstorms* (Montgomery, Vt.: Bradford Books, Reprinted by The MIT Press, Cambridge, Mass.).

Dorling, Jon (1972). "Bayesianism and the rationality of scientific inference," *British Journal for the Philosophy of Science* 23:181–190.

Doyle, Jon (1979). "A truth maintenance system," *Artificial Intelligence* 12:231–272.

Doyle, Jon (1980). *A Model for Deliberation, Action, and Introspection*, MIT Artificial Intelligence Laboratory Technical Report 581.

Doyle, Jon (1982). "Nonmonotonic logics," in *Handbook of Artificial Intelligence*, Paul R. Cohen and Edward A. Feigenbaum, eds. (Los Altos, Calif.: William Kaufmann), vol. 3, 114–119.

Dworkin, Ronald (1977). "Hard cases," in *Taking Rights Seriously* (Cambridge, Mass.: Harvard University Press), 81–130.

Fodor, Jerry A. (1983). *Modularity of Mind* (Cambridge, Mass.: MIT Press).

Foot, Philippa (1967). "Abortion and the doctrine of double effect," *Oxford Review* 5, 5–15.

Franklin, Benjamin (1817). *Private Correspondence I* (London: Colburn).

Gentzen, Gerhard (1935). "Untersuchungen über das logische Schliessen," *Mathematische Zeitschrift* 39:493–565. Translated in *Collected Papers of Gerhard Gentzen*, M. E. Szabo, ed. (Amsterdam: North-Holland, 1969), 68–113.

Glymour, Clark (1980). *Theory and Evidence* (Princeton, N.J.: Princeton University Press).

Goldman, Alvin I. (1967). "A causal theory of knowing," *Journal of Philosophy* 64:357–372.

Goldman, Alvin I. (1978). "Epistemology and the psychology of belief," *Monist* 61:525–535.

Grice, H. P. (1957). "Meaning," *Philosophical Review* 66:777–788.

Grice, H. P. (1969). "Utterer's meaning and intentions," *Philosophical Review* 78:147–177.

Grice, H. P. (1972). *Intention and Uncertainty*, British Academy Lecture (Oxford: Oxford University Press).

Grover, D. L., Camp, J. C., and Belnap, N. D. (1975). "A prosentential theory of truth," *Philosophical Studies* 27:73–125.

Hacking, Ian (1979). "What is logic?" *Journal of Philosophy* 76:285–319.

Hare, R. M. (1952). *The Language of Morals* (Oxford: Oxford Univerity Press).

Harman, Gilbert (1973). Review of Roger Wertheimer's *The Significance of Sense*, *Philosophical Review* 82:235–239.

Harman, Gilbert (1974). Review of Stephen Schiffer's *Meaning*, *Journal of Philosophy* 71:224–229.

Harman, Gilbert (1976). "Practical reasoning," *Review of Metaphysics* 29:431–463.

Harman, Gilbert (1977). Review of Jonathan Bennett's *Linguistic Behaviour*, *Language* 53:417–424.

Harman, Gilbert (1980). "Reasoning and evidence one does not possess," *Midwest Studies in Philosophy* 5:163–182.

Harman, Gilbert (1982a). "Conceptual role semantics," *Notre Dame Journal of Formal Logic* 23: 242–256.

Harman, Gilbert (1982b). "Logic, reasoning, and logical form," in *Language, Mind, and Brain*, Thomas W. Simon and Robert Scholes, eds. (New York: Erlbaum), 13–19.

Harman, Gilbert (1983). "Human flourishing, ethics, and liberty," *Philosophy and Public Affairs* 12:307–322.

Hempel, C. G. (1960). "Inductive inconsistencies," *Synthese* 12:439–469.

Hempel, C. G. (1965). *Aspects of Scientific Explanation* (New York: Free Press).

Hempel, C. G. (1966). *Philosophy and Natural Science* (Englewood Cliffs, N.J.: Prentice-Hall).

Herzberger, Hans G. (1982). "Naive semantics and the liar paradox," *Journal of Philosophy* 79:479–497.

Horwich, Paul (1982). *Probability and Evidence* (Cambridge: Cambridge University Press).

Humberstone, I. L. (1971). "Two sorts of 'ought,' " *Analysis* 32:8–14.

Jeffrey, Richard C. (1969). "Statistical explanation versus statistical inference," in *Essays in Honor of Carl G. Hempel*, Nicholas Rescher, ed. (Dordrecht, Holland: Reidel), 104–113.

Jeffrey, Richard C. (1981). *Formal Logic: Its Scope and Limits*, second edition (New York: McGraw-Hill), chap. 7.

Jeffrey, Richard C. (1983). *The Logic of Decision* (Chicago: University of Chicago Press).

Kahneman, Daniel, Slovic, Paul, and Tversky, Amos, eds. (1982). *Judgement under Certainty: Heuristics and Biases* (Cambridge: Cambridge University Press).

Kneale, William C. (1956). "The province of logic," in *Contemporary British Philosophy*, H. D. Lewis, ed., third series (London: Allen and Unwin), 235–262.

Kripke, Saul A. (1975). "Outline of a theory of truth," *Journal of Philosophy* 72:640–715.

Kyburg, Henry (1961). *Probability and the Logic of Rational Belief* (Middletown, Conn.: Wesleyan University Press).

Lacey, A. R. (1976). *A Dictionary of Philosophy* (London: Routledge and Kegan Paul).

Lakatos, Imre (1970). "Falsification and the methodology of scientific research programmes," in *Criticism and the Growth of Knowledge*, Imre Lakatos and Alan Musgrave, eds. (Cambridge: Cambridge University Press), 91–196.

Levi, Isaac (1967). *Gambling with Truth* (New York: Knopf).

Lewis, David (1969). *Convention* (Cambridge, Mass.: Harvard University Press).

Lewis, David (1975). "Languages and language," in *Minnesota Studies in the Philosophy of Science*, Keith Gunderson, ed. (Minneapolis, Minn.: University of Minnesota Press), vol. 7, 3–35.

Malcolm, Norman (1963). "Knowledge and belief," in *Knowledge and Certainty* (Ithaca, N.Y.: Cornell University Press), 58–72.

McCarthy, John (1980). "Circumscription: A form of non-monotonic reasoning," *Artificial Intelligence* 13:27–39.

McDermott, D., and Doyle, Jon (1980). "Non-monotonic logic I," *Artificial Intelligence* 13:41–72.

Meyer, Robert K. (1971). "Entailment," *Journal of Philosophy* 68:808–818.

Miller, George (1956). "The magical number seven, plus or minus two: Some limits on our capacity for processing information," *Psychology Review* 63:81–97.

Nagel, Thomas (1970). *The Possibility of Altruism* (Oxford: Oxford University Press).

Nisbett, Richard, and Ross, Lee (1980). *Human Inference: Strategies and Shortcomings of Social Judgement* (Englewood Cliffs, N.J.: Prentice-Hall).

Peirce, C. S. (1877). "The fixation of belief," *Popular Science Monthly* 12:1–15. Reprinted in *Philosophical Writings of Peirce*, Justice Buchler, ed. (New York: Dover, 1955), 5–22.

Pollock, John (1979). "A plethora of epistemological theories," in *Justification and Knowledge*, George Pappas, ed. (Dordrecht, Holland: Reidl), 93–114.

Popper, Karl (1947). "Logic without assumptions," *Proceedings of the Aristotelian Society* 47:251–292.

Popper, Karl (1959). *Logic of Scientific Discovery* (New York: Basic Books).

Ramsey, Frank (1931). "Truth and probability," in *Foudnations of Mathematics and Other Essays* (London: Routledge and Kegan Paul), 156–198.

Rawls, John (1971). *A Theory of Justice* (Cambridge, Mass.: Harvard University Press).

Raz, Joseph (1975). *Practical Reason and Norms* (London: Hutchinson).

Reiter, Raymond (1980). "A logic for default reasoning," *Artificial Intelligence* 13:81–132.

Ross, Lee, and Anderson, Craig A. (1982). "Shortcomings in the attribution process: On the origins and maintenance of erroneous social assessments," in *Judgement under Certainty: Heuristics and Biases*, Daniel Kahneman, Paul Slovic, and Amos Tversky, eds. (Cambridge: Cambridge University Press), 129–152.

Schiffer, Stephen (1972). *Meaning* (Oxford: Oxford University Press).

Searle, John (1983). *Intentionality* (Cambridge: Cambridge University Press).

Sellars, Wilfrid (1963). "Some reflections on language games," in *Science, Perception, and Reality* (London: Routledge and Kegan Paul), 321–358.

Shoesmith, D. J., and Smiley, T. J. (1978). *Multiple-Conclusion Logic* (Cambridge: Cambridge University Press).

Simon, Herbert A. (1969). *Sciences of the Artificial* (Cambridge, Mass.: MIT Press).

Sosa, Ernest (1980). "The raft and the pyramid: Coherence versus foundations in the theory of knowledge," *Midwest Studies in Philosophy* 5:3–25.

Stalnaker, Robert C. (1984). *Inquiry* (Cambridge, Mass.: Bradford Books/MIT Press).

Stebbins, Sarah (1980). "Necessity and natural language," *Philosophical Studies* 37:1–12.

Steiner, Mark (1978). "Mathematical explanation," *Philosophical Studies* 34:135–151.

Tarski, Alfred (1956). "The concept of truth in formalized languages," in *Logic, Semantics, Metamathematics* (Oxford: Oxford University Press), 152–278.

Unger, Peter (1975). *Ignorance* (Oxford: Oxford University Press).

von Neumann, John, and Morgenstern, Oscar (1944). *Theory of Games and Economic Behavior* (Princeton, N.J.: Princeton University Press).

Wertheimer, Roger (1972). *The Significance of Sense* (Ithaca, N.Y.: Cornell University Press).

Williams, Bernard (1980). "Internal and external reasons," in *Rational Action*, Ross Harrison, ed. (Cambridge: Cambridge University Press).

Ziff, Paul (1972). "What is said," in *Semantics of Natural Language*, Donald Davidson and Gilbert Harman, eds. (Dordrecht, Holland: Reidel), 709–721.

Name Index

Subject Index

◻◻ Bradford Books